Waste
Matters

Faces from a Yorkshire textile mill
still run by one family
after more than a century

By Roger Davy

This book was edited, designed
and published in 2010 by

Caroline Brannigan
1 Atkinson Avenue, Richmond,
North Yorkshire

www.carolinebrannigan.com
01748 821041

ISBN 978-0-9562965-6-6

Printed in the UK by the MPG Biddles Group
Bodmin and King's Lynn

For Barbara
Jeremy, Rebecca, Elizabeth and Kate
and their families

Foreword

O ur Company, The Bradford Waste Pulling Co. Ltd, was founded in 1895 by my grandfather, Francis Henry Davy. He was born at Kildwick near Keighley, West Yorkshire, in 1862 and lived until 1929. The business still thrives today, albeit in a vastly different form from that created by my grandfather. It has survived two world wars, the depression of the 1930s and three major recessions in the woollen industry.

At the beginning of the twenty-first century, two of Frank Davy's great-grandsons preside over the organisation. Although not large, it can now be described as worldwide, with operations in the United States and China in addition to the original base in Bradford, West Yorkshire.

Working at T' Waste Pullin', as it was known locally, meant processing all types of textile wastes, mostly in a form of spun threads, which were produced during the spinning or weaving process. These wastes were delivered to us from other textile mills or from waste merchants who bought the material from the manufacturers and our company recycled them into a valuable product that could be re-used within the textile industry. For example, for 80 years or more the company processed large quantities of fine wool thread wastes which, when subsequently processed by a specialist felt maker, ended up as felt for piano keys and as surgical felts. We processed vast amounts of waste from the manufacture of cloth to cover tennis balls.

Other processed natural fibres such as mohair, alpaca and camel hair were blended with new fibres of the same type and re-spun and woven. We were commission processors and charged so much a pound, or later a kilo, for each blend processed.

All the fibres were new and unused and our business should not be confused with 'shoddy', which is produced when old clothes and fabrics are broken down and turned into a lower quality product which might end up as donkey-jackets or carpet under-felts.

A glossary of textile terms is included at the end of this book.

The natural fibre trade with which I was most familiar is virtually at an end and now my nephews Andrew and Mark are processing and merchanting synthetic fibres such as para-aramids and meta-aramids for use in motor clutches, brake linings, protective linings for firemen's uniforms and the sails of ocean-going yachts.

I retired in the early 1990s, having spent a working lifetime with the family firm. Although I do not miss the daily hurly-burly and, in more recent years, very difficult economic times, I certainly do miss the people with whom I was in daily contact. This includes the customers and in particular the people who worked for us, some for 40 years or more. These words and pictures are dedicated to them.

This is a personal record of a way of life within our family business, of a place, processes and ways of working which have mostly gone for ever, not just in Bradford, not just in our well-loved West Riding of Yorkshire, but throughout the length and breadth of our land. The story is the same in all areas of heavy industry where large concentrations and generations of people grew up, lived, and spent their lives working in the same industry and often for the same firm.

For the most part, the folk who came daily to work F' t' Waste Pullin' were good and faithful men and women who served us well.

As for me, I grew up amongst them and was happy to work alongside them. I also had the real privilege to meet, throughout our kingdom, customers and suppliers who became personal friends. I am eternally grateful to all of them, for that long family business experience and for the way so many have ultimately cheered and enhanced my life.

R.D.
Ilkley, West Yorkshire
November 2010

Ghosts

One Friday evening during winter in the mid 1970s, I was making my usual inspection of the mill when everyone else had gone home. Even if staff were due to be working on the Saturday morning, this was something I always did on my own for peace of mind before leaving for the weekend, making sure that all was well and the buildings secure.

I had walked through the strangely quiet sheds, the remnants of steam in the heating pipes causing intermittent metallic coughs. I opened the heavy sliding door into the bottom shed and turned on and off a few lights as I walked along. I turned right into the dark passage towards the wash-house, slid open the two fire doors and put on the lights.

The scouring bowls had been cleaned and refilled ready for Monday morning, the floor had been swept and a wisp of remaining steam rose from the boiler gently warming the cold water. I carried on down the passage beside the bowls and checked that the internal inspection lights in the dryer were switched off. This was the routine.

I reached the end of the room by the sloping conveyor belt and was about to turn back when I had the absolute feeling that I was not alone. I turned quickly and looked back down the room and I know I saw a figure standing by the wash-bowl hopper. The figure was looking my way but in that split second I could not discern any features except that he, and I believe it was a man, was wearing a long overcoat, almost to the ankles, of the fashion that was worn in late Victorian England.

Now I am not prone to invent stories and I had no real feeling of fright or concern but I am convinced of what I saw then. It happened on at least two other occasions in roughly the same place and always in the wash-house when I was on my own in the evening. I do not believe I imagined this and I have often wondered if I did in fact catch momentary glimpses of my grandfather Francis Henry Davy. I rather hope I did.

Our family textile business, The Bradford Waste Pulling Company, was founded jointly in 1895 by my grandfather, Francis Henry Davy, and his two brothers. These were John (1854-1942) and Stephen (1872-1941). They were the sons of William Davy, who had been born in 1828 and Mary Ann Davy, née Barrett, born in 1831.

They lived in Kildwick, between Keighley and Skipton, in Airedale, West Yorkshire. William was the local clog and shoemaker. He and Mary Ann had nine children and, with all those mouths to feed, the boys left school when they reached their twelfth birthdays and began work, part-time at first, at T & M Bairstow's mill in Sutton-in-Craven.

The company specialised in the manufacture of 'fine' woollen cloth. Fineness in this context denotes the high quality, smooth nature of the finished cloth as opposed to one that is more coarse such as Harris Tweed. Fineness also denotes the quality of the original wool fibre as it comes from the sheep. (See glossary). That specialist statement does not do justice to what a firm such as Bairstow's meant to the community. There were other mills in the village but probably half of the adults in Sutton worked at Bairstow's for most of their lives and their livelihood depended on the success of that company.

The home of my great grandfather, William Davy, was one of a small group of cottages on a bend in the old road to Skipton, opposite the parish church in Kildwick. At least three of his sons shared a bedroom in the tiny house. In the room, apart from the usual basic furniture, there was a large zinc bath, which contained, winter and summer, about six inches of cold water and a soaking wool blanket.

The zinc bath, the shallow cold water and the soaking blanket was for the sole use of the brothers. This was long before bathrooms were included in the more humble homes and so every morning, to tone each other up, the brothers would take it in turns to stand in the bath, wrap themselves in the blanket and rub each other down to stimulate their circulation. Sometimes on really cold winter mornings it was necessary to break the skimming of ice which had formed on the surface of the water before the daily ritual began.

There was a considerable difference in age between the three brothers. By 1895, when John was 41, Francis 33, and Stephen 23, all were carding, spinning or weaving 'over-lookers' in the mill, which meant they were responsible for the management and the quality of work in their departments.

Married and with growing families, they decided to take the considerable risk of leaving steady employment and branching out on their own. Those were the days of

*Left: Francis
Henry Davy
(1862-1929)
pictured in
about 1925*

*Above: Stephen Davy,
wool, waste and noil
merchant, in the 1930s*

*Left: John Davy, wool
and waste merchant,
in the 1930s*

*Sutton-in-Craven 1914 with T & M Bairstow's mill.
The village of Kildwick is on the right at the back.*

*Left: The cottage at
Kildwick, third house
down, Francis Davy's
birthplace*

*No.1 Shed in 1976, the original Anchor Shed in
1895 of The Bradford Waste Pulling Co*

the rapid expansion of the British Empire when, for people with the necessary drive, risk-taking was part of the way of life.

The brothers' ambition led to John and Stephen becoming textile waste merchants, while Francis became the waste processor. They rented property in Bradford, in Fawcett Court, near the bottom of the old Manchester Road, for sorting and storage warehouses, and Anchor Shed in Prince Street, Dudley Hill. Anchor Shed had been a Salvation Army Citadel and even in my time a local officer would still call for an annual donation to the cause.

Here they installed machinery essential to the industrial processing of 'waste,' a preparing 'knotter' machine and two garnett machines.

Garnetting is the name of a textile process using a garnett machine which is specifically designed to recycle thread waste. The machine consists of several sections of rollers of different dimensions covered with angled saw-tooth wire of varying wire density. These run at different speeds and in different directions, between which threads are momentarily held and progressively pulled apart until they are reduced to a fully fibrous form.

A few years after transforming the premises, the Davy brothers also bought a very basic scouring plant where the waste had to be hand-forked through a tank of warm water, the action causing the twist in the thread waste to relax. Then it was pushed into a mangle which squeezed out much of the water. The material was spread on wooden scrays over steam pipes to dry prior to garnetting. All this effort must have been back-breaking.

Just how the three brothers managed to fund the dramatic change from being employed at the mill in Sutton and moving to Bradford is uncertain, but they must have accumulated wealth from somewhere to accomplish the move. It seems unlikely that they would be able to do this on the wages they were paid as spinning and weaving managers, especially as my father told me that my grandfather never owed anyone a penny.

Indeed my father's advice (not heeded!) in turn to each of his own three sons was, to quote the Bard, "Neither a borrower nor a lender be". Other relatives have told me that at some point John Davy might have gone to South Africa and, possibly, speculated in the gold fields, but nobody really knows. What is certain is that they found the wherewithal to go into the textile trade.

But they must have felt there was a market to be exploited, for the branch of the industry on which Francis Davy embarked is highly specialised, requiring extensive and detailed knowledge of the characteristics of natural fibres.

Moving On

Initially, to save travelling each day, Francis and his wife, Mary Ann, with their baby son Walter, moved from Sutton to Bradford and set up home at 219 Lapage Street, in the Laisterdyke area about two miles from the mill at Dudley Hill. This was a huge environmental change from the relative countryside of the Aire valley to the crowded, dirty, smoke-laden city. Mary Ann, especially, did not settle there and eventually the family moved back to a leafier Sutton, Francis travelling daily to his work by train and tram.

Every morning, before going to Kildwick Station to catch an early train to Bradford, Francis walked up the village to feed his hens in their run at the bottom of West Lane.

Despite the potential difficulties and the obvious risk of fraternal disharmony, the three brothers shared any profits that were made over the next ten years, until 1905. They had also agreed to share any potential losses. In their circumstances it made sense and was economically sound for the three families living in Sutton or Crosshills to buy some household items in bulk and to share them out.

My father told me that this included large sacks of sugar and a railway truck of house coal, which would be kept in a siding at Kildwick Station goods yard. When fuel was needed for one of the homes, the children from each family would have the job of going to the yard with a wheelbarrow. When the truck was empty, another full one would be delivered to the sidings by the LMS railway (London, Midland and Scottish).

By 1905 the brothers must have been in a financial position to go their separate ways and each established his own company. John and Stephen remained waste merchants and Francis was confirmed into the position of waste processor at Dudley Hill.

Francis Henry, my grandfather, died in January 1929, and his eldest son, my father Walter, became managing director, a position he held until the 1970s. Dad was born on the 18th March 1894, grew up in Sutton-in-Craven, and went to school there.

He had the nick-name of 'Tush', given to him by his friend Arthur Bottomley. The name was derived from the character Goody Two Shoes as my father was the first amongst his group of friends to have a pair of fine leather boots when all his contemporaries were still wearing traditional clogs. Perhaps his grandfather William had made them for him in his Kildwick workshop.

Dad grew up in a very close village community where most of the social life was based on the local Baptist Church. As a teenager, he had a close group of friends who in 1908 formed one of the earliest companies of scouts, so early that the only uniform they had was the traditional hat worn by the founder Baden-Powell and a stout wooden stave.

As teenagers, they formed another group based on the local church which went under the wonderful name of The Young Men's Mutual Improvement Society. What the

*The young people of Sutton-in-Craven Baptist Church
1910. Walter Davy is in the back row, extreme right.*

*The Young Men's Mutual Improvement Society, Sutton
Baptist Church 1910. Walter Davy is third from
the right, back row*

young ladies of the village thought and whether they were mutually improved too by the boys I have no idea but many of those young men went off to the Great War together and sadly not all returned. Those who did eventually married and, with their brides, remained close friends for the rest of their days.

One of them, Arthur Bottomley, became head cloth designer at T & M Bairstow's mill. He and his wife Bessie became a 'courtesy' uncle and aunt to my brothers and me. When Princess Elizabeth, now Queen, was married in 1947, Bairstow's were asked to manufacture some pieces of cloth for her trousseau and Arthur created a fine woollen dress cloth in a grey/blue shade. The cloth was so fine that it could be pulled through a wedding ring but was so opaque that you could not see through it.

The beautiful soft yarn was twisted with a thread of alginate which is an artificial fibre derived from seaweed to give it some extra strength during weaving. During the finishing process, the use of warm water dissolved away the alginate and the fine wool remained. My father's cousin Mary Spencer was chosen to weave this sublime cloth and, even though it was a labour of love and skill, Mary was heard to say, "I wish that Arthur Bottomley would just stay at home!"

In the summer of 1908 my father, Walter Davy, left school one Friday afternoon in July at the age of 14 and on the following Monday morning got up early to catch the train with his father to begin work in Bradford. To enhance his knowledge, Walter also attended Keighley Technical College as a night-school student to study textiles. During term time, he had a long, tiring day.

It must have been considered a good idea for Walter to

Wages book for April 1912

*Arthur Bottomley
1910*

*4 Jackson Street,
Sutton-in-Craven,
Walter Davy's
home up to 1920*

learn all aspects of the trade with his Uncle Stephen. Stephen Davy was one of scores of waste merchants in Bradford who visited the spinning mills and bought the unwanted material. This would be taken in jute bales to the warehouse to be sorted into various types and qualities. Any rubbish would removed and the waste sold on to another merchant or sent for the recycling process.

In its reclaimed fibrous state, the wool waste would then be sold on again to a spinner or felt maker as a constituent part of a new blend.

Walter did not look back on the initial years with his uncle with much satisfaction or happiness. He told me several times that one of the jobs he hated most was when, near the end of the working day, his uncle would send him across to Hall Ings or Union Street where the ranks of haulage men and their horses and wagons would stand waiting for work. He had to try to persuade one of them to take some bales all the way up the steep Wakefield Road to Dudley Hill for his father to process. I can now imagine the colourful language that would greet his request. It was probably quite a shock to his non-conformist Baptist ear.

Almost immediately, he was also sent out with a bag of samples to try to sell sorted and processed wool to the buyers in the spinning mills. These men were rulers in their own kingdoms because it was on their experience of buying the best and most cost-effective raw materials that the ultimate success of their company would depend. Dad would travel by tram and on foot around the mills in Bradford and by train to Dewsbury and Batley, Halifax and Huddersfield.

After an age waiting his turn with other merchants in some dimly-lit reception area, he would enter the sample room and unwrap his samples from their traditional blue papers. Dad often had the humiliation of his samples being literally thrown back at him across the sample room table, some ending up on the floor, without a word being said by the buyer. He told me this was often the case at J & JT Taylor Ltd, in Batley. The following week the routine would be repeated. I am sure it was a demanding time, but some would say these somewhat brutal receptions were a good way to learn the hard-nosed attitudes within the trade.

It was in the sample room at Stephen Davy's mill, which had by then moved to a white, stone-faced building near the bottom of Bolton Road, that on one April day in 1912, Dad heard the dreadful news of the loss of the White Star liner 'Titanic', which had hit an iceberg off Newfoundland in the North Atlantic and sunk on her maiden voyage to New York, with the loss of many lives. The First World War

Walter Davy in the Royal Navy circa 1917

The minesweeper HMS Sea Sweeper, Walter Davy's ship during the 1914-1918 war

started in 1914 and the following year, in 1915, just before universal conscription was introduced, Dad volunteered to join the Royal Navy and so left employment with Uncle Stephen. It is quite surprising to learn that in order to be accepted into the Navy, Dad had to get references, which he did, from his former schoolmaster and Sunday school teacher. During the war he trained as a radio telegrapher at Crystal Palace in London and spent some time on the destroyer, HMS Christopher, based in Chatham, Kent.

He was then transferred to HMS Sea Sweeper, a trawler built in Goole, East Yorkshire, which had been converted into a minesweeper together with a flotilla of four other similar vessels. He was based at Falmouth in Cornwall, patrolling the Western Approaches, laying mines and searching for German submarines.

It was when attending the Baptist church in Falmouth that Walter met and was befriended by Ernest Moss, a master builder and prominent citizen in the town, and his wife. Walter later married their youngest daughter, Doris in Falmouth, on 19th October, 1926. Walter brought his young bride to live in Ilkley, West Yorkshire, where they raised my two brothers and myself and where they spent the rest of their lives.

After the First World War and a lengthy convalescence following a serious attack of rheumatic fever, Dad went to work with his father, Francis, in the mill at Dudley Hill. Dad's sister Olive worked in the office. After her mother died in 1922, Olive had more time and, as she had not married and presumably needed an occupation, she provided secretarial help to her father.

She travelled with him to Bradford each day from Oaklands, the family house just above the railway station in the village of Steeton near Keighley. Olive herself died in 1935 at the young age of 37.

Francis Henry Davy, my grandfather, died in January 1929, just a few days after my older brother Keith was born, and Dad became managing director. Much later, following internal reorganisation, he became company chairman.

Walter Davy in 1924

What Waste Pullin' Is All About

Waste in our section of the textile industry is a term used to describe the by-products from the spinning and weaving processes. Mills would send us these by-products to change into useful fibres which could then be sold on as a raw material to other companies to turn into something else, such as felt. In our case this was almost invariably new material and should not be confused with that used in the 'shoddy' trade, which traditionally has been based in Dewsbury and Batley, and which uses actual waste from old soft garments.

From its founding in 1895 by my grandfather, the company was a commission processor. His two brothers were the waste merchants. We provided a processing service to waste merchants and woollen and worsted spinners but did not buy or sell the material that was sent to the mill.

The thread waste was teased apart into a fibrous form, which needed specialised machinery and expert-eyed staff to keep the original fibre length as far as possible.

For example, fine white wool thread waste would be cut to say, two-and-a-half inches, blended with similar material into a large pile of perhaps two tons in weight and hand fed into a pre-opener (Laroche) machine. This pre-opening process was necessary to put the material into a half-opened state before scouring and garnetting to help to reduce subsequent fibre breakage. On the Laroche machine the material was fed between slow-running grooved feed rollers and picked up by a roller running at a very high speed. This roller was covered with many thousands of round pins, the opening action of which reduced the thread to a half fibrous state, with the appearance of a thready fleece.

Before the days of the Laroche machine, we used the William Tatham opening machine which, with a simple basic process, reduced tangled waste into a more manageable state. If the blend contained thrums, (very tight balls of threads often recovered from where a warp had been tied on to a warping beam), then the further action of a strong steel-toothed single-swift 'knotter' would be necessary.

At the end of this journey, the wool or mohair or a mixed blend of natural fibres would drop into a scouring (washing) machine which contained, in the first large 'bowl', a mixture of warm, soapy liquid, blended with sodium carbonate which helped to remove the grease. The warm-water rinse of the second bowl would remove any remaining dirt and excess oil.

A very large dryer would remove most of the moisture. In this state the wool would be pushed in wooden skeps, (large wheeled boxes) or, in more modern times, blown into storage bins. Then it went through a specific garnett machine, suitable for that particular blend, which fully opened up the threads again ready for use by whoever bought the finished product. Different fibres, especially man-made fibres, and various types of waste, needed different processes, but the natural fibres roughly followed the above description.

Three-swift Class B Garnett machine, 1950s

*Two bowl Petrie & McNaught wool
scouring machine, 1920s*

*A William Tatham cleaning waste engine
for preparing wastes*

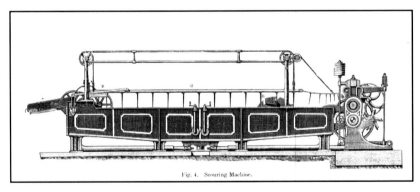

Fig. 4. Scouring Machine.

Petrie & McNaught scouring bowl circa 1914

First Memories

It was in about 1943 that I first started going to Dudley Hill. I was five years old in July that year and it was wartime. Dad used to say the mill was never busier than it was when the country was engaged in the two World Wars. Nothing was wasted and everything that could be saved was recycled.

In 1934 the company had bought two 48-inch wide cotton waste carding machines from William Tatham & Co Ltd, of Rochdale, in Lancashire. During the late 1930s and particularly when the Second World War started in 1939, those machines, and the spinning department which it fed, ran non-stop on three shifts, twenty-four hours a day, spinning pure silk noils.

These were short wool fibres cast out as waste in combing wool for worsted 'fine' yarn. The new yarn created from these leftovers was used to make shell-bags for munitions. Eventually, when this work stopped, the plant ran on ramie noils, a vegetable textile fibre, for curtain fabrics for the firm of Moygashel & Co in Northern Ireland.

In the early days of the war, my father joined the newly formed Local Defence Volunteers, later the Home Guard of Dad's Army fame. Although the Home Guard is now associated mainly with a hilarious comedy programme, these men took very seriously the task of protecting the nation under threat of invasion. All this was in the evenings and at weekends while having full-time day jobs.

Petrol for private use was severely rationed and so nearly everybody travelled by public transport, particularly by train. On Saturday mornings Dad and I would travel from Ilkley to Forster Square, the old LMS station in Bradford, and, with me holding his hand, he and I would walk up Market Street and across to Union Street at the bottom of Wakefield Road.

In those days, towards the end of the Second World War, Bradford was still a city with a heart. Mills and warehouses and good quality family-run shops jostled with one another amongst narrow streets and cobbled lanes.

Some of the shops included the family run stores of Brown & Muffs, Busby's and the stationers Tapp and Toothill's. JB Priestley, the playwright, novelist and broadcaster who grew up in Bradford, must have appreciated the name Toothill as he used it for one of his unseen characters, Tommy Toothill, in his evocative play of 1937, When We Are Married. This is set in that amalgam of West Yorkshire textile towns, Cleckleywyke, in the Edwardian England of 1908.

The leading characters, three middle-aged couples, are all celebrating their Silver Weddings. The self-made men and their wives, pillars of local society with the husbands all "big men at t'Chapel", are confronted with the news that their respective marriages might not have been legally registered. The play follows their hilarious predicament and concerns. Those characters and the way they speak remind me so much of my own Airedale uncles and aunts.

This in turn reminds me that on Christmas Day each

26

BWP price list August 1942. Some prices have been amended by sticking on an extra slip, probably to avoid the need to reprint. Paper was in very short supply at the time.

year my father, being the head of the 18 members of our extended family, would host a substantial lunch at our home in Ilkley, with roast turkey and all the trimmings. Our house would be festooned with paper streamers and after lunch we children - my two brothers and our seven cousins from Airedale - together with my mother and aunts Sarah, Anna, and Dorothy, would play party games.

My father and the three uncles, two Edgars and one Horace, not wishing to let even Christmas Day be business-free, would retire again to the dining room to sit by the fire and discuss the price of "wastes, tops and noils, cross-breds and merinos" until it was time for a slice of Christmas cake and a cup of tea. Then they all went home to spend the evening singing carols with their own chapel choirs around the big houses in Steeton and Eastburn.

In 1946, just after the end of the war, my father (together with Paul Whitaker of City Waste Pulling, of whom more anon) was recruited by the War Commission to spend a few months in Germany doing what they could, in an advisory capacity, to get the bomb-devastated German textile industry working again. The experience of seeing at first-hand the extreme devastation of war had a profound effect on both men.

They were given the honorary rank of Colonel, complete with appropriate uniform, car and driver. My father would joke about the contrast between his being a Leading Seaman Telegraphist during the First World War, a Private in the Home Guard in the Second World War and the exalted new post as an officer of staff rank in post-war Germany! I am not sure just what post-war innovations they suggested, but perhaps their written reports still exist somewhere, gathering dust on some lonely library shelf.

Bradford

I t is difficult now to realise just how different Bradford was only half a century or so ago. Even in my teenage years in the 1950s, a few horse-drawn wagons still carried jute wool bales through the busy, grubby streets. In every season there was always the lingering smell of smoky sulphur fumes in the air from the many high mill chimneys and of comforting wool grease from the scouring and spinning mills.

In the Laisterdyke area on Leeds Road, there was the sweet smell of refining lanolin from wool grease and, on hot, still summer afternoons, the pungent and sickly odours from the abattoir in Filey Street.

During the cold, damp winter months, the high concentration of smoke from mill chimneys and domestic coal fires resulted in 'smog', a mixture of fog and smoke which made travelling difficult and dangerous and caused all types of bronchial problems. I remember the density was often so intense that you could not see across the road and cars and buses would suddenly appear out of a ghostly gloom with dim yellow headlights searching for the white line.

These problems gradually disappeared after clean air

legislation was introduced but not all progress was welcome. During the 1960s, with the laudable idea of creating a new and vibrant city, much of the Victorian heart was torn out of Bradford and many well-loved buildings were demolished, to be replaced with concrete outrages which in their turn are now being removed.

Before this destruction, Bradford was still a busy, vibrant city and I still miss the old indoor Kirkgate Market, with its scores of small shops and pie-and-pea cafes, the Mechanics Institute and the glass and wrought-iron passage-ways and shops in the Swan Arcade off Market Street, where Constantine's sold fine umbrellas.

Above street level the Arcade building housed a myriad of tiny offices, each with perhaps just two chairs, a small table and a telephone for the use of the manufacturers and merchants. These offices were just a short step across Market Street from the Wool Exchange where business contracts were arranged and confirmed and ultimately honoured with just the shake of a hand. That is just how it was.

On my Saturday trips in the 1940s, Dad and I would catch an electric trolleybus in Hall Ings for the 10-minute journey from the City up the long slope to our premises in Dudley Hill. This vehicle was colloquially known as a 'trackless', and Dad would always use this word. The trolleybus, painted in the blue and cream colours of the City corporation, was a large, powerful, and almost silent means of transport. We would travel up Wakefield Road, through the busy crossroads at Dudley Hill to the stop on Tong Street, opposite Prince Street.

Bradford Corporation trolley bus for Dudley Hill and Tong Cemetery in Union Street circa 1960

Aerial view of Bradford city centre April 17th 1947

Dudley Hill

P rince Street, Dudley Hill, as I first remember it, was narrow and cobbled, paved and grubby. The street sloped gently away from the main road and low two-storey, stone-built back-to-back houses crowded on to narrow Yorkshire stone pavements on either side.

Every day from dusk the occasional cast-iron gas streetlight dimly lit the darker areas. There was a great concentration of families living in those houses in quite difficult circumstances compared with mine. Even as a small child, I could see the difference between the way of life endured there and, as I grew older, I appreciated what was my much more privileged background.

The front doors of each house opened on to the pavement and the worn door sills would be scrubbed clean each week and a holystone used to give a smart sandstone-coloured edge. Despite the difficulties, an obvious pride existed in most of the residents in trying to do their best. None of the houses had inside lavatories and there were no bathrooms. A bath would be taken in front of the fire and the primitive lavatory was down the yard.

But as in all similar parts of the city, there was a strong community spirit. The community was self-contained with all the necessary local shops, schools, pubs, chapels

No.1 Shed in the 1950s

Looking up Prince Street circa 1961 with wagons delivering 'waste'. Warehouseman Leonard Fieldhouse is pulling in a bale.

Looking over to Prince Street from Cross Bright Street after the start of the demolition of the cottages 1961

Close up of Tong Street, Prince Street and BWP 1964. The cottages have been demolished

and churches near at hand, including a branch of Midland Bank, the Co-op, and the Dudley Hill cinema which had opened for business in 1912, long before the 'talkies' came along. For many people, a visit to the city centre, perhaps to the popular Alhambra Theatre for the annual pantomime, would be something of an adventure, most of their working and leisure time being spent locally.

Our mill occupied the top one hundred yards on the right hand side of the street where it joined the main road to Wakefield and extended right through to Knowles Street. The mill buildings were a mixture of basic styles, some stone built and some constructed of red brick. The company site had evolved and grown over the years, with the expanding business being accommodated by building another shed as and when the money became available.

The original machine room had been the Anchor Shed. Later on the Imperial Shed was added further up Prince Street. The impressive name of this building came from a former occupier, the Imperial Toffee Factory. Our older employees called it, "In t' rat 'oil", or, in translation, the 'in the rat hole', as they remembered the many rodents which had been attracted to the sweet smelling company premises.

The bales of waste were usually delivered into the Prince Street yard and craned up three floors for storage and the initial cutting process. Gravity was used to start the bulky material on its journey through the mill. The blends travelled through various processes from one side of the mill to the other and the completed products were normally collected from the covered warehouse in Knowles Street.

On the left hand side on the corner of Prince Street and Cross Bright Street, John Metcalfe and his daughter

Annie ran a busy grocer's shop which they got to from their adjoining cottage home.

A black and white painted sign above the door announced that John was 'licensed to sell ale and porter, to be consumed off the premises'. The brown liquids were dispensed through hand pumps from barrels stored in the cellar beneath the shop and the customer would bring his own one pint or quart jug to be filled and taken away.

John's shop, with its scrubbed Yorkshire stone-flagged floor, had a musty aroma all its own. It boasted many brown-painted shelves from which John sold everything from jam to kindling wood. Cooked sides of bacon wrapped in muslin cloth would hang from hooks in the ceiling. Crates of metal-topped bottled 'Model' homogenised milk stood on the floor.

This milk was produced in the city at the 'Model Milk Dairy' in Sunbridge Road and was popular because it kept its freshness longer. It was darker in colour than fresh milk and had a creamy flavour in tea and coffee, but Margaret Squires in the canteen used it to make custard and memorable rice puddings.

The shop was the local source of much gossip and banter. John wore a khaki overall, and, looking back, he reminds me of the Mr Arkwright character in the 'Open All Hours' TV comedy.

Annie's friend, the wonderfully named Mrs Golightly, was often in the shop in my younger days, helping to serve but mostly joining in the general chat. She was always smartly dressed and most intriguing to me as an impressionable youngster was her hair, which was always immaculate and regularly subjected to a blue rinse. Mrs Golightly, who was invariably cheerful and chatty, almost looked out of place

*Prince Street, Dudley Hill, Bradford, May/June 1953
with the original cobbles. The BWP wagon outside
the mill is decorated for the Coronation. John
Metcalfe's grocers shop is on the corner 100 yards
down on the left. His sign can just be seen.*

in Prince Street. At one time John Metcalfe's son Geoffrey
worked in the shop too but he decided to emigrate to
Australia and subsequently made no contact with his family
in Bradford. No one knew where he was or his address. Mrs
Golightly's son, Roy, has told me that the only time there
has been contact was when Annie died and flowers arrived
with a note of remembrance from Geoffrey, but no other
details.

The shop and its occupants with its myriad of memories,
jumbled odours and echoes of cheerful sauciness disappeared
with the local cottage demolitions of the 1960s. Until 1950,

our mill office was in a three-storey building overlooking Prince Street and John's grocers shop and the mill yard. The building also contained the general office and the cutting department on the top floor. A smaller private office for Dad was in a partitioned area of the second floor warehouse. Dad's office contained a beautiful, oak roll-top desk, which had belonged to his father. It was sadly vandalised in our own joiner's shop and used to create a more 'modern' desk in the 1970s.

My brother Keith and I had a long association with the family business and, because of that, and because much of the type of work we knew so well is now no more, I decided, in retirement, to record what I remember about my day, and of the people who worked in the Company with us. I say, 'with us', because as well as being faithful employees, a good number also became close friends of our family.

Sadly, Keith died in December 2009. He was nearly ten years older than me and so was always my 'big brother'. The eldest of three sons, it was natural and no doubt expected that after leaving school he would become the first of the new generation to join the family firm. That was the way of things. I followed him ten years later. As I look back on my years at Bradford Waste it is often just the sights, sounds and particularly the smells of the old place that cause the memories to flood back so vividly.

There was the sound of someone opening the letter box at the bottom of the office stairs, and the footfalls coming up. There was the jangle of keys in the locks of the office safes and the distinctive sound when someone opened the bottom Prince Street door into the mill, followed by the clatter of heavy boots going up the stone steps into the first floor warehouse. The warm comforting smell of the wash-house comes back to me, as does the sight of the solid lumps of grease on the floor which accumulated over many months until they were scraped away. Before this annual chore, the wooden boxes would bump and jolt along as John Knight wheeled away another load of scoured wool from the dryer.

The high-pitched bubbling noise and the steam from the separate tanks which boiled up soapflakes and alkali before the brown liquid was pumped into the scouring bowls. The metal harrows of the bowls which creaked and vibrated as they pushed the sodden wool through the hot soapy water and on to the mighty sliver-covered squeeze rollers. The regular metallic clunk from the ratchet mechanism which allowed for slippage on the rollers and then the surge of liquid flowing into the metal-meshed settling tanks.

There was the constant and evocative noise of 22 large garnett machines being individually driven by heavy, wide leather belting from overhead line-shafts running the length of the sheds, with our men constantly sweeping the floor of the alleyways between the machines to prevent one type of material migrating to another.

The jangle of the steel crane hooks with their sharp teeth, as they were swung across a bale which was being loaded on to a wagon in the Knowles Street loading bay and the louder metallic noise of the hooks clanging against each other as the bale was released and the crane rope brought them in again to lift another load.

Many of the diverse group of people with whom I worked and later employed made a great influence on my life. Many spent all their working lives with us and deserve to be remembered for their loyalty and friendship. This is what I have attempted to do.

God made 'em and Walter Davy paid 'em!

Selwyn Proctor

Selwyn was a close friend of the family and had started work as the office manager in 1933. Dad knew Selwyn through being fellow members of the Baptist Church in Ilkley and to my brothers and me he was a close and respected courtesy 'uncle'. He and Dad were contemporaries.

During The First World War, because of his Christian beliefs, Selwyn was a conscientious objector. This did not mean that he avoided the horrors of France because he volunteered as a stretcher-bearer and suffered great privations on the battlefields.

Forever afterwards, and somewhat unusually for those who had served in the trenches, in any long conversation he would invariably mention one of his wartime experiences. He was wounded and gassed at the battle of Arras. Dad said you could not put a six-inch ruler anywhere on his body without touching an old wound. During his long months of recuperation he spent some time in Osborne House on

*Selwyn Proctor, our Office Manager in
the 1930s and 1940s in the uniform of
a stretcher bearer circa 1916*

the Isle of Wight. When he eventually came home to his family in Ben Rhydding near Ilkley, his lungs were badly damaged. To help his breathing, on medical advice he slept in a tent in Bolling Road School field for about two years to take advantage of as much fresh air as possible.

Selwyn was the office manager and kept the books. He was a kind and gentle man and provided good and wise support to Dad as the company steadily expanded. This was particularly so during the Second World War when the recycling of textile wastes became so crucial to the war effort. He finally retired in 1953 and as a parting gift he was given the opportunity to re-visit Canada where he had worked as a lumberjack as a young man.

Before the First World War he had intended to marry a Canadian girl, but because of his wounds and uncertain future he decided it would not be fair to her, so he did not return to Canada, and always lived with his sister Elsie, on St. John's Road in Ben Rhydding. He died aged 83 on May 18th 1976.

Walter Garside

Walter Garside joined the company in 1912 and when I knew him as a boy he was our boiler man and responsible for the Lancashire type horizontal boiler which raised steam for the wool scouring and drying plant and to heat the premises in the winter months. In the very early days before Francis Davy bought a large electric motor to run his machines, the mill was run on an extension line shaft which came into the Anchor Shed through the adjoining wall from the steam engine which ran the dye works of W & G Chambers next door. You can still see where the original hole was bricked up high up in the wall.

Walter was born in 1889 and before coming to work at the mill he had been a miner at Toftshaw colliery. He was not a tall man, but wiry and strong and had rosy cheeks and

Walter Garside circa 1940s

twinkling light blue eyes. His mother had not been happy about him working down the pit and it was his grandmother, who lived in a cottage down Prince Street, who heard of the vacancy at, as they called it, T' Waste Pullin', and got him the job.

Walter's name first appears in the company wage book on the 7th March 1912. Within three weeks he was working seventy hours a week for £1-7s-3d.

When the First World War started he was called-up and joined the Royal Veterinary Corps, working in the Horse Hospital in Abbeville. After the war he came back to the mill to work in the scouring department. He then became the boiler man and engineer and was our first wagon driver when a new Albion wagon was bought in Scotland.

Unfortunately, after being sent to learn how to service the vehicle, a few weeks after its arrival, Walter reversed it into some lavatories in the Knowles Street yard. My father decided that he was spreading his talents too thinly and his driving duties were given to someone else.

In the boiler house Walter worked in a difficult and dirty environment, hand-shovelling coal on to the boiler fire and forever watching the gauge glasses to make sure he had a good head of steam for the mill. Perhaps there was an advantage in the winter when the boiler-house would be a cosy place to be, but during hot summer days the temperature must have been unbearable.

On alternate Friday afternoons throughout the year the fire would be allowed to go out so that the following morning the boiler could be serviced and the flue pipes cleaned out. Walter's son, Bill, who was 90 in March 2003, has told me that as a boy he was always taken to the mill on Sundays to check that the boiler was in good condition to provide steam for the following morning. This means Walter was working a seven day week.

Bill also mentioned that to make sure he was not late arriving at the mill, his father had a huge alarm clock, almost the size of a station clock, to wake him each day. Bill says this machine must have woken most of the folk in Dudley Hill when it went off! On one occasion Walter, getting up early with the aid of a lit candle, set the bed clothes on fire and burnt his hands so badly in putting out the flames that he was off work for two weeks.

Walter was part of the establishment, because if no steam was generated the mill could not function properly. Scouring of the various natural fibre wastes in hot water with boiled-up soapflakes and alkali was necessary to remove spinning oil and dirt and relax the twist in the threads. This was so that the teeth on the 'garnetting' machine would not break the fibres but provide more of a combing process as the threads were reduced to an open state. Walter worked long hours and his home life must have been limited but Bill Garside said his father often took him on cycling trips around the country areas with several friends.

On one memorable occasion Walter came up the office steps in some distress. He had eaten his packed lunch as usual, on his own in the boiler-house sitting in an old wooden armchair. For some reason he always took out his false teeth to eat his sandwiches and would leave them on the paper while he munched away.

On that particular day he had screwed up the paper and, without thinking, opened the boiler fire door and threw the packet into the flames. Walter met Selwyn at the office door and confessed what he had done. "I wouldn't mind, but our Lucy will play 'ell!"

Walter was a good, faithful but rather shy and retiring, gentle man. He retired in 1954 after 42 years with the company and was presented with one of the new television sets. He died in 1966 and is buried in Tong Cemetery.

Joe Fisher

I remember Joe as a shadowy person, tall and thin, and winter and summer, before the days when overalls were provided, he always wore an open-necked shirt, walked to work in an unbuttoned raincoat and never seemed to catch cold. Perhaps because he always worked in a noisy environment, he always spoke very loudly which, as a small boy, rather scared me. He was in charge of the 'wash-house', which contained the two scouring bowls and the dryer.

During cold dark winters, because of the constant high temperature, this was not a bad place to be, but during the summer the temperature and humidity was very high and salt tablets would be offered to those who worked there to help to replace what had been lost in perspiration.

Joe lived in a back-to-back house down Prince Street without any indoor amenities and so it was not unusual late on Friday afternoons when the bowls had been 'dropped' (or emptied) and cleaned and refilled for the following Monday morning, to hear singing coming from the wash-house.

We would know that Joe had stripped off and would be sitting in the warm soapy water in the side-tank of the first scouring bowl, where the liquor was recycled, and he would be having his weekly bath. Many years later showers were provided for the staff.

I would not say Joe was an alcoholic, but probably because of his difficult working environment he liked more than a glass or two. On Fridays, with his pay packet in hand, he would usually go straight to a nearby pub and drink his money away.

Eventually his wife came to see Dad and it was arranged that she would collect the bulk of his wage so she could feed and clothe the family. Joe was given pocket-money to get him through the week. He was another of the weekly pensioners who received a 'sub' every Saturday lunchtime as my father left to go home.

Annie Bland

Annie was our first typist and came from school in 1935 to spend 13 years in our office. I can remember her washing my grubby hands in cold water in a tiny washbasin in the corner of the office after being in the mill or playing with the rubber stamps. Annie left to get married and was followed by Muriel O'Keefe.

Guy Hood

Guy was appointed cashier after Selwyn Proctor retired. He had worked in the office at Multiple Fabric Co Ltd off Cutler Heights Lane in Dudley Hill. He and Dad and Selwyn had travelled together for a long time on the train and I suppose Guy must have applied for the job when he knew that Selwyn was retiring.

There were two other applicants for the position, a Mr Appleby, and Ken Bradley, from Ilkley, who was chief cashier at the Midland Bank at Dudley Hill. Ken had been a wartime colleague with Dad in the Ilkley Home Guard and from the little I remember of him would have made an ideal successor to Selwyn but for some unknown reason

Dad chose Guy Hood. When petrol became more available Dad started going to the mill each day in our 'Lanchester 14 Roadrider Sports Saloon', (to give its full rather pretentious title), HPA 247. The car had been bought in Falmouth just before the outbreak of war and delivered to Bradford by rail, but had been laid-up for several years.

Guy had a lift too and eventually became the unofficial chauffeur. He would walk to our house, 'Kingsleigh', each morning to drive the car, leaving me at Woodhouse Grove School on the way.

Guy Hood had served for many years in the Merchant Navy as a wireless operator, and claimed to have visited every country in the world with a sea port, but eventually came ashore to what must have been a much more mundane life. Perhaps it was his many years at sea which made him appear to me rather distant and I never really warmed to him.

I always felt that he rather resented me. He was never really unkind but he married quite late in life and had no children and had little rapport with the younger generation. He was efficient enough and kept the books and every week prepared and paid the mills wages, in cash. But I came to feel that Dad should have had someone of Selwyn's character to advise him on financial matters.

When the business expanded and we needed extra secretarial help in the office, Guy could never quite cope with the young girl office juniors who often brought some brightness and cheer into the rather dull General Office atmosphere.

The mill office block is situated on the highest point of Dudley Hill. One sultry and humid summer afternoon in the late 1960s, all was quiet in the general office. Suddenly, without any warning, a thunderbolt of lightening hit the

Guy Hood Office Manager 1950s

mill flagpole that was fastened to the side of the building just above where Guy sat at his desk. The explosion was dramatically loud and the force of the strike was sufficient to break coping stones and split the long pole right down the middle and much of it fell down into Prince Street. Guy felt the surge of electricity through his body and he suffered some shock for which we administered an extra cup of sweet tea. Luckily he did not suffer any further hurt but it was a close run thing.

Guy Hood stayed at the mill far too long, but that was our fault. He was nearly 70 in 1975 before I was given the job of suggesting that it was time he retired. Guy, until only a few years before he left, kept the books using a dip pen and an inkwell but then again I imagine most offices were still run along similar lines. When he retired, the carpet around his desk was replaced as it was covered with ink stains where he had flicked his pen.

Every Friday lunchtime Guy paid the wages through a narrow hatch at the bottom of the office stairs. All the employees would stand in the passageway which ran under the offices and Guy would hand out the pay packets at spot-on five minutes to twelve. Above the hatch there was for many years a grubby card on which was the just discernible instruction, 'All sick, lame, and lazy queue here!'

Everyone knew to the final half-penny how much was due in the packet and how many hours had been worked and the amount that would be deducted in tax. No one was ever slow in coming forward to remonstrate with the cashier if it was considered there was a mathematical error!

Harry Batty

Harry came to work at the mill when he left the Army in 1945. He was born in Ilkley, the son of a chauffeur and a housemaid who had worked for a well-to-do family in a big house, 'Hollycroft', at the top of King's Road. Dad had known Harry from when he had been a boy in the Sunday School at the Baptist Church where he had been his teacher.

In due course Harry went off to the war and served in the Royal Army Medical Corps, eventually landing in

*Harry Batty with Walter and Doris Davy
at a company wedding 1960*

France only two or three days after D-Day. He acted as a messenger at that stage, carrying information to and from centres of action and various company headquarters. To do this dangerous work, often under fire, he had been provided with a large and cumbersome 'sit-up-and-beg' bicycle to help him.

The war, unreasonably, did not follow recognised roads and lanes and after several days trying to negotiate ploughed fields, he threw the bike into the bottom of a hedge and delivered his messages on foot. I think he had a 'good' war and was demobbed as a sergeant. He loyally supported the British Legion and often attended the Albert Hall reunions in November. Alan Titchmarsh, the gardener, writer and broadcaster grew up in Ilkley and writes about 'Uncle' Harry in his autobiography. He was a close family friend. In the book Alan describes Harry and his lifestyle in some detail but says, "I've no idea what he did for a living". I was able to write and tell him that Harry worked for our family firm for over 25 years.

When Harry left the Army and came home to Ilkley my father offered him a job in the mill office. I think Dad's idea was that Harry might eventually succeed as office manager, but he never quite achieved the financial expertise to do so. He could do the bookkeeping and the wages, but I think he was fairly content with his lot and not very ambitious.

He and I got on very well through a mutual interest in local theatre and we travelled to and fro each day to Bradford in a small Standard Ten van that I was allowed to use. Harry and I often worked together if there was a rush job to do in the cutting department, he feeding the machine, and me down below treading the bale.

When the bale was full Harry would go off and have a smoke until another empty bale was slung. Harry was an elegant man and smoked a cigarette with style. He was always immaculately dressed and even at work wore a long

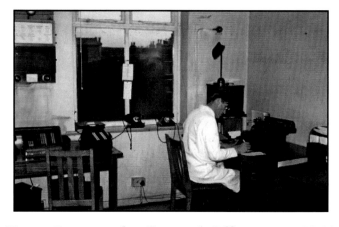

Harry Batty in the General Office circa 1961

white overall jacket that was always starched and never appeared to attract any dirt. He was our first-aid person and as well as applying neat bandages, he was incomparable in wrapping parcels and sample packets for posting.

He was a good friend and we had many laughs together. He was in his element chatting and laughing, particularly with the ladies, and if there was another, more private side of his life, he kept it to himself, not allowing it to impinge on the many other friendships he shared.

Harry left the mill in 1972 when we were in the midst of the first real textile recession in Bradford after the Second World War and sadly before I had any responsibility for staffing and went to work for the Yorkshire Electricity Board in Otley.

He was still there when he had his final illness soon after playing the heavenly visitor in the musical 'Carousel', with the Ilkley Amateur Operatic Society at the Kings Hall in the town. He died in 1974.

Lynn Woods

Lynn came to work with us in the general office in 1961. Lynn was responsible particularly for producing the individual blend sheets which detailed the various processes through which material would pass after arrival in the mill.

As we were commission processors, we charged a price to our customers for the actual work we did and, from our point of view as well as for our customers, it was very important to

Lynn Woods in the office 1976

Lynn Woods and Geoff Halsall 1976

keep an accurate account of the finished processed material to compare it with the incoming weight.

We had constant arguments with some of our canny clients who maintained there should be no loss in weight during processing but when many blends arrived with a high percentage of spinning oil on the fibres, (up to 10% on some crossbred threads), and when we scoured down to approximately 0.5%, the loss had to be justified. We did add up to 3% of water soluble oil after scouring but many clients chose not to accept their loss and sometimes even accused us of filling an odd bale to dispose of later.

Lynn would produce the blend sheets, a different colour for each process. Blends are various fibre components ultimately processed into a unified form.

This meant Lynn had the inconvenience of separating each of five copies with a sheet of carbon paper. With the variety of work we used to do there could easily have been 20 or 30 different blends on the premises at any one time, those arriving, those in work, and those ready for collection.

Accurate paperwork was essential and Lynn accomplished this arduous responsibility faithfully, cheerfully and well. She also acted as a private secretary for my father, Keith and me, and when I became managing director I depended very much on her confidentiality and advice.

She brought an attractive femininity to the male orientated general office. Lynn worked with us for 21 years and the company and the Davy family owe her sincere thanks for her loyalty and, not least, her good humour.

Geoff Halsall

Geoff arrived as a breath of fresh air into our family business in the middle of February 1975. He and I had been friends for several years and when I heard that he was leaving his position with BOCM the animal feed producer in East Yorkshire where he had been a farm management advisor I suggested to him that he might like to join us when Guy Hood retired.

Geoff immediately brought the office management up to date and created a more contemporary way of bookkeeping and budget control. This was important not only to the parent company but to my brother Keith's emerging position as a textile merchant. Geoff was a great asset to Keith but even more to me as I did not have much financial expertise and I knew I could depend on Geoff to give me sound honest advice and cheerful support.

I was pleased in due course to appoint Geoff a director of the company in appreciation for the responsibilities he assumed. His only vice, if you could call it that, was going to mill sales. However, the result of this was that many times he saved us large sums of money by bidding for items which he felt "might come in useful sometime".

Across the 12 years he worked in our office, I can remember him buying the contents of a joiners shop from a mill in Laisterdyke, barrels of oil and sacks of soda ash and detergent used in the scouring department and even a flagpole and Union Jack. Over the years he must have saved us thousands of pounds in raw material costs. Geoff moved on in 1987 to work for Pennine Fibre Industries in Denholm.

Angela Reynolds

Angela worked in the general office from being a teenager until she had her own family. She was a cheerful and conscientious young lady and did wonders in keeping my desk empty of paper rubbish. We really missed her when she left to have a family.

Lynda Chisholm

Lynda (pictured below) came to work with us as Lynda Swales, straight from school in Tong, and I remember her diminutive figure coming up the office stairs with her mother for her interview as our office junior. Eventually Lynda married Andy and now has two daughters, Hollie and Georgia. After nearly 25 years she is still faithfully helping my nephew Andrew with his international business.

Fred Smith

Fred Smith was the works manager for most of my younger days. He was a Scotsman from Dundee, who had served his time as a young man in the jute mills in India and began work at the mill in 1936. He was recruited initially to supervise the running of the Tatham carding machines and the accompanying spinning machines. He was efficient and would stand no nonsense.

In his spare time he became an Alderman on the town council in Cleckheaton, and was closely involved with East Bierley Cricket Club in the Bradford league. To denote his status he always wore brown overalls during working hours rather than the usual washed-out blue worn by most of the men and it was he who would plan the work for the various departments.

When new staff were needed in the mill, he was delegated to do the interviewing and appointing. In my younger days he was kind to me and as he had no children of his own rather enjoyed my company. As the years went on he became, perhaps understandably, a little more 'crotchety', in a similar way to Guy Hood.

Perhaps he rather resented the younger generation taking more responsibility in the family firm. Fred eventually retreated to the works garage and would frequently be found there, sitting on an old bentwood chair in front of a one-bar radiator, with his head in his hands, a half-smoked cigarette nearby. He, too, was 70 before I was again given the difficult job of suggesting that he should retire, which he did in 1974. His retirement was marked by the presentation of a large silver salver, commissioned by the family and made by my brother, Peter, who by this time was well established in teaching, having qualified as a silversmith via the Colleges of Art in Bradford and Manchester.

Fred was 85 when he died in 1989 and I have just been in contact after many years with his widow Ethel who is still in East Bierley and was 99 in August 2010.

It may seem strange that we allowed two old retainers to stay so long in the company, but this was not unusual in

Fred Smith, works manager, is back left, Albert Foulds, machine minder is front centre and Alf Miller, is back right, in the mill 1970s

Bradford and perhaps the two men were a little afraid of retirement. It was not in my father's nature, if he could help it, to dismiss loyal employees. Dad, of course, worked full-time until he was 69 and did not stop coming to the mill on a regular basis until he was 76. I think that Fred and Guy used that as an excuse that Keith and I allowed to run. In retrospect I believe that we were wrong to do it. Work had continued to come in on a regular basis during the 1950s and 1960s and the mill was busy, but it was the first of the big textile recessions and the three-day week in 1971 which made us look at last at the manning levels and how the mill could be made to work more efficiently with more up to date ideas.

Cllr Fred Smith in his robes as an Alderman at Cleckheaton 1960s

My Early Days At Waste Pullin'

Going back to my early career at the mill, after my schooldays were over I went in the late 1950s to the Textile Department of Leeds University for three years to study for a diploma in textile industries. It was open to men and women from all over the world who wanted to learn the rudiments of textile processing.

I had worked at the mill in the holidays for years, from being an early teenager, but now life became more serious and I was put on the payroll for about eight pounds a week. I created something of a problem for my father and eldest brother, who didn't know what to do with me. The problem was compounded in 1961 when I joined the company as a full time employee.

My father had no thoughts of retiring. The word 'retirement' was not in his vocabulary and most weeks he would work for five and a half days. That changed after Dad had a serious accident when helping in the mill on September 3rd 1963 and lost three fingers in a converted gill-box, used for breaking down wool tops.

He took several months to recover, not least from the shock, and it was then that he started to come to the mill less often. It was the catalyst that made him step back from the running of the business that had been the main interest in his life since 1908.

Until that happened, I was wondering what on earth I was going to do in a family business where my father and eldest brother were firmly established and the organisation on a daily basis was the responsibility of two old retainers.

I was young and naïve. I think that it had always been assumed amongst family and friends that, as the younger son, I would join the family business. Those were the days before careers teachers advised school-leavers about what they would like to do, or discover what interested them. So without any discussion and without any real personal thought, I drifted into life at the mill.

I have always quietly admired my brother Peter who from the first showed no interest whatever in the family business and struck out into teaching. Many years later I believe that if it had not been for my influence and responsibilities, the processing side of the business would not still be there. Sometimes in a nostalgic moment I wonder if I had been more studious and academic and expressed an opinion on a future career, whether I would have made a good naval officer?

But instead in the summer of 1957 I readily accepted the suggestion that when I was not in Leeds I would work on the machines in the mill wherever I was needed. This was the best grounding I could have had. I worked in all the departments and did not mind getting hot and dirty and I learnt to work alongside an interesting and (mostly) cheerful and faithful group of men and women, whose upbringing had been so very different from my own.

I broadened my experience of life and learnt about many of the work and domestic problems of those whom we

Roger Davy with the Italian FOR carding machine 1976

employed. Eventually in the summer of 1961, when I began full-time working, no specific role in the company had yet been devised for me by my father and brother. So, as we were building and fitting out the new No.3 shed, I started to work in our maintenance department with Stanley Jessop. So began several years close association with one of our most faithful employees.

Left: Roger Davy helping to demolish a Knowles Street shed 1961

Below: Walter Davy in his office circa 1960.

Stanley Jessop

Stanley started working at the mill in the early 1950s
when he was employed by the Cleckheaton joinery
business of Beaumont and Smith's. There was no full-
time joiner at the mill and so Dad had to employ outside
help. Eventually Stanley was working so regularly at Dudley
Hill that he was invited to join the staff and have his own
joiner's shop, which was situated above the warehouse in
Knowles Street.

The area, many years before, had been used as a Salvation
Army Hostel and where Stanley had his workbench had
been a cottage bedroom where one of our employees in
Francis Davy's day, Johnny Burns, had been born.

I was assigned to Stanley's care and thus began a strong
mutual friendship as we worked together for the next few
years. Stanley retired in 1981 by which time my experience
within the company had widened enormously, I had
assumed far-reaching responsibilities and become managing
director.

On the day he left I presented him with a gold watch,
and in my few words to the assembled mill folk, I quoted
the words used as a memorial to Sir Christopher Wren at
St Paul's Cathedral in London, 'If you seek his memorial,
look around you', because they were appropriate words to
describe the quality of work created by Stanley within our
company over many years. That same day I drove Stanley

home to 'Boundary House' in Church Lane in Gomersal where he lived with his wife Amy. There were tears in my eyes as I left, as I felt it was the end of an important chapter in the long story of our firm.

I really wondered how we were going to manage without him and his friendship and support. I do not think at this stage I can do better than quote from the letter I wrote to his family after we heard the sad news of Stanley's death in 1994.

"Amy, for weeks I have been meaning to contact you to see if it would be convenient to come to see you, but it does sound that you have been having a difficult time, and perhaps this is the time to remember my old friend as I really knew him, not only as a work colleague, but as a true and good friend.

The Davy family as a whole will never be able to adequately repay the great debt we owe to Stanley. For as nearly long as I can remember he was a good and faithful friend to us at the mill at Dudley Hill, and in many different ways at our various homes.

When I arrived at the mill to work full-time in 1961, as the younger son, it was not easy to find me a suitable job or responsibility and so I was given to Stanley as his labourer, and he and I worked together for the next three or four years.

Although I already knew that Stanley was a skilled craftsman, I shall always appreciate the times I spent with him and saw those skills in action. There seemed to be nothing he could not do. Apart from his wonderful work with wood, he was an excellent plumber and electrician, and at repairing drains, digging foundations, repairing

Stanley Jessop in his joiner's shop 1976

Left: Pte Stanley Jessop 1940, probably taken before embarkation for France.

Below: Stanley Jessop coming ashore after his rescue from the French beaches May 1940

Left: Oak lectern made by Stanley Jessop in 1979 in Ben Rhydding Methodist Church

roofs, and building walls he had no equal. I must admit
that he was very jealous of his various skills, and I was
not allowed to do much fine work, but as a fetcher and
carrier I learnt a lot.

Stanley was a great conversationalist too, and as we worked together he would regale me with all sorts of stories of his time at Beaumont and Smith's, his time in the Army, of days out on Wrekin Hill in Shropshire, and all sorts of experiences such as being at Scapa Flow during the war, building barracks, and of sending home packets of butter in the hollowed-out boilers of toy wooden trains he made in his spare time.

He also told me of being on the beach for five days at Dunkirk in 1940 and of standing in the sea for hours waiting to be picked up on the nearby beach at Wimereux between Boulogne and Calais.

I am convinced that he appears in a piece of film that the BBC incorporated into a drama-documentary they made about the Dunkirk evacuation. A young Stanley in khaki battledress is seen walking down a gang-plank arriving back in England.

Some time ago when we visited her in her home in Batley I showed some 'stills' from the film to Amy. She was not convinced, but I think I am right. I have since shown the photos to Sandra, Stanley's daughter and she says she is happy for me to include the Dunkirk photo in this book.

Stanley was a good Anglican and attended St Mary's Church in Gomersall where he did all types of maintenance and much of the work when a Lady Chapel was added in the nave.

In a quiet moment he also confided to me that he had

become frustrated when cutting the grass in the churchyard about the number of very old gravestones that were in the way of the mower.

With the permission of the then vicar, Rev Donald Aldred, he moved a few to a different and more convenient area. One day when he was working there a group of visitors from the Bronte Society arrived to inspect the grave of Mary Taylor who had lived at Red House in the village and often entertained in her home, her friend Charlotte Bronte. Although the gravestone still exists, little did those visitors realise that the particular patch of grass they inspected did not contain Mary's remains!

My letter to Amy continued:
'There were also many times when I was at the wrong side of Stanley's circular saw as we cut timber. The dust would invariably blow into my eye, and I was very much the 'under-dog'. I particularly remember the summer of 1959 when my brother Peter and his wife Libby moved to Thornton Rust, near Aysgarth, in Wensleydale, and Stanley went up there to work for a few days.

Every day for a couple of weeks Stanley would load up our little Standard van with cement, timber, plaster-board and tools and send me off on a round trip of over a hundred miles with the front wheels nearly coming off the ground because of the weight in the back.

When I pointed that out to him he would just say "Oh you'll be all right, come and get another load tomorrow!" I actually did all those trips without mishap, but it was touch and go.

Later on when my father stopped coming to work

full-time, and I became MD of the processing side of the business, it was Stanley, on whom I could absolutely rely to do a first-class job. He would look for a job, get on with it and finish it properly.

My father and Stanley also enjoyed a friendship which was special between them, because there was no barrier or awkwardness, just a mutual respect. I remember that they once went to a sale of timber and bought a beautiful plank of oak and it was put into safe storage until a worthy use for it came along.

The oak was still stored above Stanley's bench in the joiner's shop when my father died, and in his memory I asked Stanley to use the wood to make a lectern for use in our Methodist church in Ben Rhydding. He did so and the lectern has always been admired and is a worthy example of Stanley's craftsmanship.

The lectern is based on one I took Stanley to see which is in daily use at Woodhouse Grove School. It has two small plaques recording the names Walter Davy and Stanley Jessop. It is used at every church service and it is also a splendid memorial to my father whose life it commemorates, and to his friend, the craftsman, who designed, carved and constructed it. The lectern was dedicated in our church in Stanley and Amy's presence in December 1979.

On Friday, 28th August, 2009 my wife Barbara and I went to Amy Jessop's funeral in the Parish Church of St John at Carlinghow, near Batley. We were told by Amy's niece, Joan, that Amy had been in failing health for a little while and had decided she would not have any further treatment.

She had her ninetieth birthday on the second of May in that year. After the touching and memorable service we were able to speak to Stanley and Amy's daughter Sandra

71

and her husband Brian, and to their son, Dean, of whom his grand-parents were very proud. Dean drives main-line trains between England and Scotland.

So ended another generation of friendship in the history of our Company.

Wilson Hool

Wilson was a legend in his own lifetime. I do not know anything of his younger days except that he had been a miner, but the harsh working life had been difficult for him and he left to drive a van for J Edhouse & Co who were fishmongers in Bradford. He came to work at the mill in 1936 as the lorry driver. When war broke out in 1939 Wilson was called-up and served his time in the Royal Electrical and Mechanical Engineers.

He returned to the firm when he was demobbed and whether he learnt his wily ways in the Army or whether it was always part of his nature, Wilson was one of those rare people who could obtain things that were in short supply or down-right impossible to get! He was built like a tank, not tall, but immensely strong. My brother Keith remembered when he was nine or ten years old, how Wilson would get into a crouch position and Keith would sit on one of his hands, with my brother Peter on the other, and the two of them would be lifted high into the air.

From my earliest days I knew Wilson as our wagon driver and he would spend his days driving around Bradford and

Wilson Hool 1976

*Wilson Hool roping up the wagon in
Prince Street circa 1962*

the West Riding mill towns collecting and delivering bales to and from our customers. As a boy I would sometimes go with him and on one memorable Wednesday afternoon when I had a half-day holiday from the Grove, I was picked up at the bottom of Westville Road in Ilkley and taken to a mill in Skipton to collect a load of wicker skeps (baskets) containing bobbins of yarn to be 'garnetted'.

As Billy Foreman, another employee, had come to help with the loading, I had to sit on the metal cover over the hot engine in the cab of our Thorneycroft lorry with only a piece of sacking to protect my bare legs from being burnt. The highlight of the afternoon for me was stopping at the green-painted transport café in Draughton where Wilson bought me an enormous bacon and egg sandwich which I seem to remember was as big as my head!

My father depended on Wilson in many ways and again, like the relationship Dad had with Stanley Jessop, there was a strong mutual respect between them. Wilson could work wonders with car engines and kept the family vehicles in good order. He stripped down the Lanchester Saloon, and rebuilt the engine after it had been laid-up during the war, including removing jellified petrol from its inner workings. Later on when the bodywork continued to crumble away he replaced the offending areas with pieces of cocoa or dried milk tins before re-spraying the area.

Wilson never asked the company to buy him a new wagon rope to secure the bales. He managed for years to 'find' ropes that had been lost from other wagons and fallen into the road ready for him to retrieve.

Wilson lived with his wife Sarah and daughter Lillian on Tong Moor at Birkenshaw. Until the early 1950s most food items were on ration but Wilson created a little sideline to supplement his family's needs by keeping pigs. At that time there were strict regulations about keeping animals, as meat was rationed, but I believe that Wilson had an arrangement with the local constabulary or at least with one member, to turn a blind eye in return for a share of the benefits.

It was illegal to dispose of animals without going to a recognised slaughterhouse, but Wilson had built his pigsty against a convenient wall bordering the local railway line and when it was time for an unfortunate animal to be moved on, Wilson would wait for a train to pass and shoot it with a .303 rifle. Where the rifle or the ammunition came from I really do not know, nor do I wish to enquire, but after all this time I believe that our family may have been offered and accepted some crackling.

One illustration of Wilson's ability to satisfy unusual requests occurred in the early 1960s. My mother, father and I had visited some close family friends in Sweden in 1959 and on our return my father had the idea of sending the Bagge family a present. A literal translation of the word 'bagge' into English is ram, a male sheep, so Dad decided he would like to send to Sweden a stuffed and mounted ram's head. But where would he find one?

Wilson Hool provided the answer. After making the request a few weeks passed, and Wilson then came to the office and said, "Mr Davy, I've found you a ram's head". Dad said, "Well, where is it?" and Wilson told him, "Still running around on Silsden Moor!" After another few days, Wilson came up the office stairs carrying a large polythene bag containing the head of a magnificent animal with large curly horns. Stanley Jessop had already been primed to make a suitable box and the bag and its somewhat bloody contents was packed up with shavings, labelled and sent off

The ram's head obtained by Wilson Hool

on the afternoon train to a taxidermist in London. After another couple of months the stuffed and mounted head was delivered back to Bradford and eventually arrived in the small harbour town of Skelleftehamn on the Gulf of Bothnia in the far north of Sweden. The harbour master took delivery but could not understand the custom import documents which stated that the wooden box contained 'machine tools'. Evidently, a 'ram's head' could indicate engineering spares.

Wilson continued with the company for several years after his lorry driving days were over and he worked part-time until he was 70 looking after our very large Italian FOR carding machine. Wilson was another person who was utterly loyal and dependable and a close friend of the family. Sadly, Sarah died first and Wilson lived in a flat in Birkenshaw until his final illness in the 1980s. I still miss his company and cheerful chat.

Frank Whitaker

Frank was the first works engineer that I remember. He had been a boyhood friend of Dad in Sutton, and they were boy scouts together when the movement was first founded in 1908. At the outbreak of the First World War Frank joined the Royal Navy as an engine-room artificer and served his time as an engineer, particularly on the battle cruiser HMS 'New Zealand' and served at the Battle of Jutland in 1916.

One of the stories Dad told me about Frank's navy days should be recorded. During the war, one of the young midshipmen who had responsibilities in the engine room was Prince George of Battenberg (1892-1938), the brother of Lord Louis Mountbatten. Prince George came to Frank one day in the huge engine room of the 'New Zealand'. He had various records to keep during his watch and he asked Frank how it was possible that the number of revolutions per hour of each of the two mighty propeller shafts running from the two separate engines were almost identical? Frank said, "Come with me Sir".

They went to the gauge that recorded the number of revolutions of one of the engines, wrote the figures on a piece of paper, then scrambled across the engine room to the other gauge. Frank checked the paper with the second gauge, then lifted up the gauge glass and then manually moved the figures with the ratchet until they were almost

Above: Model horizontal steam engine made by Frank Whitaker, BWP engineer, for Walter Davy

Right: Frank Whitaker 1910

Left: HMS Sea Sweeper kettle stand made by Frank Whitaker for Walter Davy in the 1950s

identical. Frank said, "That's how we do it, Sir!" After the war Dad offered Frank the job at the mill and he remained there for the rest of his working life. He was responsible for all the engineering work and spent his days in the mechanics shop, which was reached by climbing steep wooden stairs above the garage near the Knowles Street yard. The 'shop' had a lathe, large drilling machines, a mechanical saw and a two-stone grinder for sharpening knives and 'fettling' tools. There was also an anvil, and a blacksmith's forge, but I do not remember the latter being used much.

The whole atmosphere smelt strongly of iron filings, paraffin and grease. Near the top of the stairs there was always an old bucket full of dirty black paraffin and soaking in it an equally old brush, handy for cleaning a piece of grease-laden machinery or ball-race brought up for repair. In the corner was a vertical mechanical drill where as a boy I spent many hours drilling holes in pieces of wood.

Nearby were two steps which led to a door on to the flat roof over No.2 shed. At the side of the steps was a narrow wooden bench, built over some steam pipes and long enough for two men to sit on. The site was popular in winter and summer as a meeting place for generations of mechanics and 'over lookers' where gallons of tea would be drunk with toast and buttered long-bun tea-cakes from the nearby cafés.

Frank Whitaker with his melancholy face was often to be found there. Dad used to tell the story of how worried Frank had been throughout his 53rd year because his father had died at that age. It was only after his birthday came around again that Frank confessed that he had got his own age wrong, he was going to be 55 and not 54 and he had worried for a whole year for nothing! Frank cannot have been busy with mill work all the time because he managed to make a large horizontal model steam engine complete with copper boiler to produce the steam to drive it. I still have the engine and remember Dad bringing all the parts home and making the engine come alive by putting the boiler on the gas stove to heat the water. Our kitchen became full of the delicious smell of hot oil and steam. Frank also had a sideline making heavy fire pokers with decorative handles. I wonder how many are still in use in West Yorkshire?

Frank was a craftsman and anything he made was very solid and would last for ever. One summer, in an attempt to make it easier to cut the grass at home, Dad asked Frank to convert our push-and-pull lawn mower, by fitting it with an electric motor to drive the cutter cylinder.

The motor was powered from the mains with an electric cable about 50 yards long. Frank did what he was asked but the resultant machine was so heavy Dad could not even push it!

Frank had some sadness in his family life, in that his only child, a daughter, at the end of the war married a German soldier who had been a prisoner-of-war in England. The marriage was a happy one but Frank could never accept his son-in-law. He personally felt humiliated, perhaps because of what his country had twice suffered during his lifetime.

Frank retired through ill health in the early 1950s, left a comfortable home in Sutton-in-Craven, the village where he had lived all his life, and moved with his wife to a remote wooden bungalow on a hillside high above the road between Coniston and Ambleside in the Lake District. He did eventually move into Ambleside but died only a few years later. This was a sad ending for a gentle man who had great engineering skills and considerable creative talents.

Johnny Burns

Johnny was a cheerful man who by the time I knew him was almost ready for retirement from his work in the warehouse. He and Walter Garside were the only employees I knew who had been employed by my grandfather. Johnny told me that Francis Henry was a stickler for keeping his staff fully employed and on the job.

On one occasion, when there was a shortage of work in the mill, everyone had been set on to re-whitewash the walls and ceiling in No.1 shed. Johnny was at the top of a high ladder when he dropped his paint brush just as Francis walked into the shed. Johnny was just setting off down the ladder to retrieve the brush when Francis asked him where he was going. His explanation carried no weight with his boss. Francis told him to stay where he was and threw the brush back up to him.

Johnny's mother, Mrs Burns, worked in the wash-house for many years, feeding the wash bowls while wearing a long black dress with a grey apron over it and a piece of hessian cloth over that to protect her from the dirt and grease.

Fred Abbott

Fred was another warehouseman whom we employed for a number of years after Johnny Burns retired. Fred worked with Leonard Fieldhouse and shared the tasks of receiving and sending out the many bales of fibre that were processed week after week. Fred reached his potential early on in his career at the mill, but, although he

Fred Abbott 1976

was willing enough, he never looked for a job and would always wait for instructions.

He was invariably cheerful, but had only one speed, which was very slow. The only time you saw Fred break into a trot would be at the end of the working day as he crossed Tong Street on his way home. This increase in activity was merely to avoid being knocked down by rush-hour traffic. Fred's wife Ada also worked for us for some years in the cutting department. She was a quiet but cheerful woman.

Billy Foreman

Billy was our maintenance man when I was a boy. There is not much to tell, but he had been a former miner who had worked as a bricklayer in the open-cast coal mine on the land at the bottom of Prince Street and Knowles Street.

Initially the coal used in our boilers came from this open-cast mine. I particularly remember Billy because he was responsible in 1940 for building the air raid shelter at the back of 'Kingsleigh', our family home in Ilkley.

It had a blast-proof entrance and a stove and an escape hatch, just in case the main exit became impassable. I do not think the family ever used it, but I can remember being held tightly by my mother as we crouched under the stone slab of the store cupboard in the larder, presumably when there was an air-raid alert. How well Billy built the shelter I am not sure, but after the war it was converted into a garage, and it is still standing, 70 years later.

Noble Clough

Noble came to work at the mill after the war. He lived in one of the mill houses facing on to Tong Street. He was foreman in the cutting department where 'waste' was cut to reduce its overall tangled mass, prior to preparing and scouring.

Precision cutting of wool and speciality fibre 'tops' was also carried out. Noble was a chap who just got on with job. He had a quiet personality but ran his department efficiently, and had skill in setting and sharpening cutting blades.

The cutting department employed a variety of ladies over the years, for example Margaret Squires, Alice Milner, May Wales (whose husband had a haulage business) and Annie Welch. All four ladies had originally worked in the spinning department. It was invariably a cheerful area and was always clean. It had to be, to prevent the contamination of very valuable materials.

Over the years we cut many thousands of tons of high quality wool tops for Paton and Baldwin's, the internationally renowned manufacturers, to a length of an inch and a quarter, the cut sliver falling down through a trap door into a new jute bale slung from the ceiling of the floor beneath.

There someone would literally tread the bale until it weighed about 150 kilos, pack it as tightly as possible, then fix the top of the bale in place by sewing with very strong string or by or using wooden skewers to do the same job. The whole area had the distinctive, comforting smell of combed wool and jute.

The ladies who worked there were a cheerful, homely group and there was continuous banter all day. They wore no specific uniform but they would wear a working dress - no lady wore trousers in those days - and a full length apron. At Christmas-time they decorated the room with streamers.

The ladies' only responsibility was operating the cutting machines and ensuring smooth progress. Noble Clough would maintain the machines and change the blades. Being the only man in the department he had to have a broad back to withstand all the saucy banter that was directed at him from all sides. In later years Noble was succeeded by Joe Preece and then by Dennis Walker.

Looking back, to my young inexperienced eyes, Annie Welch was the most worldly of all the ladies, wearing plenty of make-up and rather over-powering scent, even during working hours.

There were strong rumours of her having a liaison with another of our employees, but it would indiscreet to say who it was believed to be.

Annie died over 50 years ago and my brother Keith went to the funeral where the mourners were asked to meet at the family home before the service.

On arrival he was disconcerted to find that, in a manner then traditional in parts of the north of England, the open coffin was still in the front room, with Annie on view for all to pay their last respects!

Frankie Jackson

Frankie was a tiny man, not much more than five feet tall. I am not sure when he came to work with us but I believe it must have been in the 1930s. He is the only person that I have met who saw Bradford City win the FA Cup Final in 1911. (Bradford City 1- Newcastle United 0, after a replay).

Frankie normally worked on the garnett machines in either No.1 or No.2 shed. In the late 1960s the strenuous work became too much for him and he was used for odd jobs around the mill, including packing bales in the cutting department. One hot and sultry summer afternoon I was passing the entrance to the Laroche room above the scouring department and noticed that material falling down from the big cutter on the floor above was overflowing the bale and falling on to the floor. I assumed that Frankie had gone off to have a smoke or to make a mug of tea and I climbed the bale steps to push the material down.

You will understand my shock when I discovered Frankie unconscious under the cut material. He had fainted in the humid conditions. It was a good job I found him when I did. Dennis Walker and I managed to get him out, brought him round, gave him a drink and took him home. He was back again next day and carried on. Frankie had the brightest, most cheerful, twinkling blue eyes of anyone I can remember.

Margaret Squires and Alice Milner

These cheerful ladies became the company cooks when the works canteen was first opened in the 1940s in one of the cottages we owned off the Knowles Street yard. Here everyone would have a good hot lunch every day.

Dad and the office staff would go upstairs to what had been a bedroom to have their meal. I remember the stone flagged floors and the walls being covered with large ornate oil paintings, being part of my grandfather's collection which had somehow ended up there.

The paintings were sold in the late 1950s and I believe the subject matter of Highland cattle knee-deep in a misty Scottish loch and late Victorian English portraits were then so unfashionable that the frames were the most valuable part of the sale. It would be different now.

Later a new canteen was built, together with a mill store, above No.2 shed. In that kitchen Margaret would cook memorable lunches, and the quality of her Monday Yorkshire puddings has never been surpassed. They were of course eaten on their own with thick onion gravy before the main course. The waistlines of my father and brother were never the same again.

Once, when my mother was confined to bed with a very bad attack of fibrositis, the housekeeping at home was thrown into some confusion. To help supplement the evening meal, my father quite innocently offered to bring home a 'Dudley Hill Tart' the offer of which has gone down as a gem in our family folklore.

For the sake of the record I must also mention Margaret's bilberry pie and custard. Wonderful! She was a good Catholic and went to mass every day, and treasured a small bottle of water from the River Jordan that my mother-in-law had brought home from a holiday.

She would tell droll stories about her family and one I remember involved her daughter for whom Margaret had saved-up for months to pay for her to have singing lessons. During the night following the first lesson the gentleman singing teacher unfortunately died and Margaret blamed herself for months afterwards saying it must have been because of the poor quality of her daughter's voice!

Alice Milner was a small, very round lady and she moved from the cutting department to help Margaret in the canteen but Alice was not a very good cook.

She did the more mundane jobs such as peeling the potatoes and washing up and twice a day would walk through the mill with a large stainless-steel jug of hot steaming tea, which everyone would buy at an old penny a pint. Alice was quite capable of opening the large sliding door to No.1 Shed, and bawling (there is no other word for it) "Tea up!"

She would easily be heard above the considerable noise coming from 10 garnett machines. We rather dreaded Alice being in charge of the canteen when Margaret was away because the quality of the meals really suffered.

Alf Miller

Alf Miller became the works engineer after Frank Whitaker retired in the early 1950s. He was not one of my father's best appointments. Alf came from P & C Garnett's in Cleckheaton. Garnett's were the machine makers who gave their name to a textile process, 'garnetting' which is the ultimate process used to reduce waste threads to a fully fibrous state.

The design of the machine is similar to a carding machine but has more 'working' parts. Placed around half of the circumference of the fast-running swift are eight slow-running 'workers' rotating in the opposite direction with the rollers covered with metallic saw-tooth wire of differing angles.

The threads are held between the swift and worker and the action gradually reduces the thread to its ultimate fibrous state with as little fibre breakage as possible. The 'doffer' roller would transfer the material from one working part to the next and a doffing comb would finally remove the material from the machine. Depending on the type of thread waste to be reduced to its fibrous form, the garnett machine used would have anything between two to five swift and doffer sections.

There were many different machines at the mill for processing the wide range of 'wastes' from coarse carpet threads to the finest botany wool. I believe Alf Miller had not been a great asset to Garnett's but he had served his time there and we needed a trained engineer. We tolerated his laid-back attitude far too long. He would never offer to go the extra mile and even in the middle of an emergency which might have the mill at a standstill, he was known to just go home. No doubt this was his right but I could never warm to him.

I always knew when he was going to be away because he had the habit of putting his tools away the night before he rang in to report that he was ill. He ate huge quantities of mint imperials, so much so that he used to grind down his false teeth. When this happened I have seen him take out his denture and use a small file to put on a new biting edge. I was very thankful when he at last retired in the early 1970s and moved down south.

Leonard Fieldhouse

Leonard had worked before the war for one of our customers, Fred Bairstow and Co., in Fitzwilliam Street. After serving in the RAF there was no place for him in the two-man business and Mr Bairstow asked Dad if he could employ him, so Leonard joined us in 1947 as our warehouse man, responsible for all the many blends of material which came and went every week.

Leonard was a slight man, always well groomed, wearing clean blue overalls every Monday morning. He worked from his headquarters, a small cabin in the Knowles Street

Leonard and Mary Fieldhouse in the 1970s

warehouse where he had a wooden desk and a stool and various warehouse books that contained all the details for every blend of material being processed through the mill at any one time.

A blend sheet was created by Lynn Woods in the office from the weights of the individual bales as they arrived on the premises and the sheet would contain the processing instructions for the blends as they passed through each department - cutting, preparing, scouring and garnetting.

Leonard was meticulous in his work. He had to be because he was ultimately responsible for every pound and later every kilo of material that we processed. We had to be able to justify the out-going weights of each blend against the weight of the material coming onto the premises.

The waste merchants of Bradford and the West Riding were a canny lot and often they were not prepared to accept that there would be a 'loss' of weight during processing through oil, which had been added during the spinning process, being scoured out when the blend was washed, Weight could also be lost through fibres breaking and falling out as 'droppings' during carding or garnetting.

It was not uncommon for us to be accused of keeping material, so creaming off any profit that a customer might expect. Often with the cross-bred or coarser natural fibre blends of thread wastes, or alpaca, or camel hair, there could be up to 15% of spinning oil or natural grease on the threads or fleece when they came in to us, which was removed in subsequent processing. Dad always called the oil, the 'fatty-matter' content.

In addition to the oil added after scouring to prevent subsequent fibre breakage, the only way to try to give the customer some compensation for loss would be to allow some 'condition' to remain when the processing was completed.

We would aim at perhaps not more than 2.5% water content. If there was a larger amount we could be accused of creating a situation where mildew could cause a slimy and evil-smelling disaster. This was particularly possible with speciality fibres such as mohair or alpaca fleece which could rapidly heat up and, through spontaneous combustion, even catch fire if left un-touched in a pile on a hot summer day.

Some customers were not averse to taking our blends back and, in their own warehouses, opening the bales and laying the garnetted blends on special floors covered with mesh grills under which were tanks of water. Having been left for a week or so, this would allow moisture to be absorbed into the fibre which would then be re-baled and re-weighed before sending the finished product to their own customers.

Any sensible buyer would ask for the blends to be tested and a certificate of worthiness produced by the Bradford Wool Conditioning House before accepting the order. The Conditioning House certificate with its red seal was recognised and accepted throughout the world.

Leonard Fieldhouse was such a perfectionist that often he would become quite agitated and wonder how he was going to cope when he had perhaps three or four wagons queuing-up in Prince Street to be unloaded. But he always did cope. I can still see him plainly now, as he pulled on the friction-crane rope to lift a bale from a wagon in the Prince Street yard. As it took a little strength to do this, he would invariably coil his foot around the rope to give some extra purchase.

When the bale reached the crane door bay it again took some strength and often some courage and skill to swing the bale out and, just when it swung in again with its own momentum, pull the crane rope just enough to safely land the bale on a bale cart for wheeling away. When all was safely gathered in and each bale had been weighed and accounted for, he would take the incoming delivery note to the office with a brisk step, his steel two-spiked hand-hook hanging and bouncing from a loop on the back of his overalls.

Leonard looked after the paperwork for many years. He retired in 1969 and died in 1992. He had a long and a happy retirement, caravanning around the country and riding his tandem bicycle with his wife Mary, who taught dressmaking skills in night schools in Bradford and specialised in creating beautiful embroidery.

The last time Leonard and I met was outside Morten's hardware shop in Ilkley, two or three years before he died. He greeted me like a long-lost son and grabbed me and gave me a hearty kiss on the cheek! He was another faithful 'Waste Puller' whom I remember with great affection. I discovered recently that Mary Fieldhouse is living in a retirement home in Ben Rhydding and I have let her see what I have written about Leonard.

Arseeni Veemees

I find I have little to say about Arseeni because he was a bachelor and lived on his own in the Manningham area. He said very little but just got on with his job on the garnett machines quietly and efficiently.

I was the only one to speak to him using his first name. In our mill he was always called 'Jimmy' or 'Jimmy the Pole'. His actual home country was Estonia and he had come to this country in 1945 after working in forced labour camps in Germany.

Subsequently he discovered that he had no village or family to return to and decided to make a new life in England, eventually coming to live in Bradford. Before the war, Arseeni had worked as a guard on the Estonian railway, a position of some seniority, but I presume the extreme privations that he suffered for five years and the fact that his native land was now occupied by Russia had affected his spirit and he was content just to stay where he felt safe.

Arseeni Veemees with hand-rolled cigarette 1976

Arseeni worked hard and faithfully and I can still see him leaning on a wall near the Prince Street lavatories having a regular smoke. He rolled his own cigarettes and kept all the constituent parts for the process in a tobacco tin. There would be some loose, strong tobacco, cigarette papers and a little machine to roll everything together. The resultant cigarette was always very slim and he would appear to smoke more paper than tobacco. I can see one now, never firm and straight, just very thin and bending in the middle as it hung out of the corner of his mouth.

Arseeni retired when he was 65 in the middle 1980s. Sadly I have lost contact with him but I hope he has had a long and happy retirement.

Dennis Walker

D ennis came to us in about 1960 after working for some years for Reinhard Hensel, a textile waste merchant who had premises on Thornton Road in Bradford. I shall write more about Reinhard later. Dennis had served his time in the Navy during the latter part of the war and his elder brother was a Lieutenant Commander diver for most of the years that Dennis was at the mill.

I believe that Dennis often regretted leaving the service as a Seaman Petty Officer but his wife Margaret was in poor health most of their married life. Being loyal to her, and wanting to care for her, he never had the chance to go back to sea and so spent the rest of his working life with us. My father, in his usual quiet way, often gave extra financial support to Dennis to help him to raise his four children. Dennis was in charge of the cutting department after Noble Clough retired and so was responsible for constructing the various blends of material as they started their processing journey through the mill.

I should mention that very few blends of 'waste' contained just one type of material but, more often than not, they were made up of perhaps six or seven different types of thread which had to be blended together in the cutting and preparing stages so that there was a uniform product at the end.

Sometimes, particularly when processing several different shades of alpaca, Dennis would have to supervise the blending in a similar way to an artist mixing his paints on a palette. Too much or too little of one shade could compromise the final required blend.

We worked for many years for Edgar Heap Ltd, a company in Sunbridge Road which sold, amongst many other types, scoured and carded alpaca blends to a manufacturer in the south of France weaving alpaca cloth for ladies wear. Heap's director, Horace Giles a most genial and kindly man, would come to the office week after week with a sample basket containing just a few ounces of several types and shades of alpaca fleece.

It was my job for many years to scour and then process the small amount through a sample carding machine, to make sure Mr Giles had the correct proportions before he committed us to producing perhaps two tons of a finished blend.

Dennis Walker and his helpers would place all the constituent bales around an open trap door and throw down on to the blending floor in the room beneath a little

Dennis Walker in the canteen 1976

of this type and a bit of that and a person underneath would spread it all out and build up the pile until it often touched the ceiling. Those working on the 'Tatham' preparer would then cut into the pile from top to bottom in proportion, pulling off armfuls of fleece, and place it on the feed sheet of the machine.

By the time the material had gone through this process and the two-bowl scourer and had been blown into a storage bin by a very powerful fan, the blend was well and truly mixed together.

This brief description does not do justice to the care and skill involved in getting the blend just right. I remember, too, that Edgar Heap's blend numbers were 1544 and 1547 and these lots were repeated month after month. Horace Giles had to continuously achieve the same shades for the repeat orders. Again, much skill was required.

As well as Edgar Heap's French customers, these blends were often sold to Henry Wheatley Ltd, in Mirfield, and Keith had a very fine overcoat made from some of the cloth created from these blends. I suspect like many other skills in the Bradford trade, this special skill for blending is now largely lost.

Dennis Walker became one of our most dependable employees and was responsible for all the initial work on the blends going through the mill. Like Walter Garside, he would usually come on the premises seven days a week to make sure that all was secure.

We were in his debt. Dennis was a widower for many years after Margaret died in the 1980s and he himself died in 2001.

John Knight

J ohn deserves a chapter to himself. He worked with us for nearly 30 years from 1960 until he had to retire early through ill-health in December 1988. After working for Garnett's of Apperley Bridge for 10 years, John moved with his mother to a house at the bottom of Hall Lane and then looked for work a little nearer home. He was 'set-on' by Fred Smith to pack the bales of cut material from the cutting department.

I hope John would not mind me saying that he was one of our employees who never achieved status as a charge hand, or had great responsibility within the company, but he was one of those faithful men who spent many years with us, who did their work well day by day and enabled the business to carry on efficiently and produce quality processed material that was readily accepted throughout the textile world.

After several years of working as a packer for the wool top-cutting department, John moved downstairs to work with Charlie Mason in the scouring department, wheeling away wooden skeps of dried material to storage bins throughout the mill. In 1975, Pneumatic Conveyors Ltd of Huddersfield installed a 'blowing' system, which efficiently moved the various materials around the premises.

The engineer who came to do that installation was helped by our friend Fredrik Bagge from Sweden who came

John Knight, Dennis Walker & Arseeni Veemees 1976

for six months to work with us in the mill. There was a bonus in this new system in that the material which might have become a little matted during scouring was released and opened as it passed through the fan, making it ideal for the carding or garnetting process. Fibre breakage was also greatly reduced.

John was almost the first person on the premises each day and because he could not get used to dentures he did not appear to eat much, but I know he believed he was in paradise when in the mid-1960s we installed a vending machine which dispensed coffee, tea, and hot chocolate.

The machine accepted three-penny bit coins, and John must have spent a fifth of his wages on hot drinks, especially coffee, so much so that word went around the mill that on one occasion when he had to go for a blood test, all the nurse could find was "Maxwell House". John was subjected many times to taunting by some of our younger and more insignificant employees and would threaten to leave. It was usually my job to sort things out. He could shout very loudly and describe in graphic detail what he intended to do to the perpetrators, but he was gentle soul at heart and I could calm things down without too much trouble.

Sartorially, John was never ideally dressed for work and he was someone who really benefited when, in the 1970s, freshly laundered blue overalls were provided weekly for everyone, including me!

One of the pleasurable things I did for John was to organise a few holidays for him. One day he came to me and said that he and Willy Evans wanted to go abroad. This came as something of a surprise from two chaps who to my knowledge had never been much further than a day trip to Harrogate, or fishing in the canal at Apperley Bridge. John and Willy were adamant that they wanted to see something different, so I contacted a travel agent friend of mine in Bradford and explained the circumstances.

In 1981 and '82 they went to Spain, but then a year or so later for some reason they decided they would like to go to Germany. My friend came up with the suggestion that the two of them should go via ferry to Hamburg on a five-day trip from Harwich. This would include two nights on the boat and the trump card was that when the ferry reached Germany there was a small hotel within 200 yards of where the boat tied up at the quayside.

This was ideal because neither of the intrepid travellers had a word of German and I knew they would not want to go far. And so it was. Somehow they got themselves to London, then to Harwich on the boat-train which took them to the quay where the ship was waiting and they sailed away on their big adventure. I admired their courage. When they arrived safely home again we could see from their photographs that they had not strayed more than a quarter of a mile from the hotel and the photos were of a young lady hotel receptionist. But they had been to Germany.

When in 1985 he completed 25 years with the company, I was delighted to present John with a gold watch, which I was frequently told kept perfect time for many years. Through ill health, John retired in December 1988. He was one of those people who could raise your spirits at difficult times and would always have a cheerful word as we passed each other during the working day. We enjoyed regular phone-calls, "Hello Roger, John here!" and occasional meetings in Bradford over a cup of coffee when we talked about the old days. I would like to thank him sincerely for his loyalty and friendship.

There is a rather sad postscript to my account of John's time with us at the mill. At the end of May in 2009 I heard that after a three week stay, John had died in the Royal Infirmary in Bradford. This was a bit of a shock because at the end of our fairly regular telephone chats I always said that he should let me know if he was in any particular need of help. It seems that, despite medical help and home visits by the district nurse, his circulatory system had given up at last.

But that was not the end of the story. John would have told the hospital authorities that he was Johnathan Edwin Knight as that is what he liked to be called but he was actually John Edward Knight. Naturally there was no record of such a person in the Bradford records. Eventually it was confirmed that he had been born in Welwyn Garden City. After two months a copy of his birth certificate was obtained and it was possible to start to tie up all the loose ends.

I spoke to Keith Parkin who had befriended John after his natural father had died and who was accepted in the position of next-of-kin. Eventually the service was held on the 27th July. I asked Keith Parkin if I could say a few words at the funeral service at Scholemoor Crematorium about my memories of John when he worked for us. This I did for the small group of friends who met there with my wife Barbara and me. I found it an emotional experience but I did not want John to leave without tribute being paid to him for his long time service to the company and for his friendship down the years.

*John Knight and Willy Evans on holiday
in Hamburg circa 1980*

Willy Evans

Willy worked with us for several years in the 1970s and 1980s. When he first came he was called Willy Barber. He was a machine minder and not very clever technically but he would carry out any job to the best of his ability. He was a good time keeper, always very polite but had to be pointed in the right direction.

At the end of each day he would have done what was asked of him and then go quietly home, walking up the street in his swaying, gangly style. He worked on the garnett machines but would cope with most areas of work. He was certainly one who benefited from the weekly supply of clean overalls. Whether it was in the heat of summer or during colder winter days he always wore a knitted woollen hat, pulled well down.

His leisure time was often spent with John Knight and I have described how I arranged for them to have continental holidays together.

I think it was during the spring of 1986 that Willy came to see me in my office one day and said, "Roger, will you stand up with me?" I asked him to repeat the question as this was an unusual request to say the least. He said again, "Will you stand up with me?" He then gave me the surprising news that he had decided to get married and he wanted me to be his best man. I was totally taken aback because of all our employees Willy was one of the two or three most unlikely to travel down the matrimonial road. It seems that he had met a lady who was separated from her partner and who had a young daughter. Perhaps Willy saw this as a rare opportunity to be a husband. After a lengthy chat he was adamant that matrimony was just what he wanted and so I agreed to 'stand up' with him.

The appointed Saturday morning arrived and Barbara and I went into Bradford and met Willy, very smart in a suit, and his fiancée and her daughter outside the Register Office in Manor Row, together with about 20 other well-wishers, many of whom were carrying their weekly shopping in Morrisons plastic bags.

We all went in and I was able to support Willy at the happy ceremony. The wedding party then adjourned to the RAF Club in Fitzwilliam Street for the reception. As the wedding had been held soon after 10am, we arrived at the club not more than an hour later. After sitting down and chatting for another hour it became apparent that there had been a mix-up with the caterers because there was no food on the premises. Eventually telephone calls were made to Bingley to see when the sustenance might be expected.

The pork pies and sandwiches arrived at about 2pm, by which time most of the guests were completely inebriated through drinking on empty stomachs. Jimmy Gould, who was a guest and smartly dressed for the nuptials, was particularly merry and kept cheerfully coming to speak to Barbara and me, wishing us well through a rosy, boozy haze.

When it was appropriate to do so, we left the party which was in full swing, making our farewells to Willy and his new bride. Barbara asked him innocently whether they were going away, and Willy equally honestly said they were going home for an hour later on, then coming back for the rest of the evening. I think he had a week's holiday but then he was back with us at Dudley Hill.

I mentioned that Willy changed his surname whilst he was with us. I arranged that officially for him through deed poll because he had a 'Barber' cousin who was a bad lot and not unused to court appearances for various petty crimes. When he wanted an alibi he would often use Willy's name. Willy eventually got fed-up with this and took the decision to change his name.

As far as I know, Willy is still married to the lady but left our employ in the late 1980s. I would really like to know how he is getting on.

Jimmy Gould and Willy Evans 1976

Bronislaw Siedlecki

Bronislaw, or 'Ronnie' as he was always called by those who worked with him, came to work at the mill in 1972. He had worked for Paul Whitaker at The City Waste Pulling Company for several years and when that company closed down, Mr Whitaker asked my father if he could employ some of his men.

Those who joined us were all very good, conscientious workers and included Clarrie Bates, who became our highly skilled engineer, Ben Rhodes, and Willy Sutcliffe, as well as Bronislaw.

He had had a difficult time during the war years and subsequently arrived in England as he had not been able to return to his native Poland. During his time at City Waste he had a serious accident in which he lost part of his right arm but this did not prevent him from working very efficiently. I have been in contact with him and through his daughter, Wanda Davies, I asked him to let me have a short account of his life before he arrived in England. The following is what he dictated.

'I was taken from my home in Poland by the Germans at the start of the war and was taken to a German farm where I was made to work on the land. I spent two years there where I was made to work very hard although I did receive fair treatment from the family with whom I

Bronislaw Siedlecki 1976

had to live. I could not leave the farm and everywhere I went I had to have my papers with me which were checked regularly by the German soldiers.

When I was liberated I went to work with the American Army in Germany where I was stationed at an American camp, where I stayed another two years. I worked in the cookhouse preparing and making meals for hundreds of American soldiers. After my time there I was given the offer to relocate to England, Canada or America. I chose England because it was nearer to my homeland and gave me the best option to return home in the future should that opportunity arise.

Although I have visited my relations many times in Poland over the years, I have made England my home. I met and married my wife Marie and brought up two children. I hope the above is some help in composing your book and I look forward to seeing the final edition.

The retirement of engineer Clarrie Bates 1985. I have tried to identify as many people in this photo as possible. Apologies to those whose names, or surnames, have eluded me. Front, l-r: Lynda Swales, Angela McCready, Clarrie Bates, Roger Davy, Dawn Robinson and Roger's niece Barbara Davy. Second row, standing, l-r: John Sinclair, joiner, Chris, Trudy Prime, Stella Pudney, Angela Prime, Mark Davy, Ivan Zap, Dennis Walker, Alan Dickinson. Back row, l-r: Trevor Richmond, Steven Walker, Alan Richmond, Andrew Davy, John Knight, Haneef Kalif, (unidentified), Tommy Richmond, (unidentified).

When Bronislaw came to work at our mill he was in charge of two of our largest garnetting machines, Nos.1 and 2 in No.1 Shed. These four-swift machines ran constantly on fine, coloured botany wastes, often for E M Fleming & Co in Bradford and Ely Garnett & Sons in Elland. After preparing and scouring, the material would be garnetted through these finely clothed machines in such a way that we did our best to retain as much fibre length as possible.

During this process, short fibres would drop out of the machine and, if possible, be returned with longer fibre to ensure that the final product provided a decent return for the customer. It was part of Ronnie's skill that when the blend was completed there would invariably be just a small mound of droppings that could not be re-used. He would be mortified if there was a substantial amount of waste to throw away. I can see him now lying down on the floor outside the machine safety-guards, using his artificial arm as a rest as he carefully used a brush in his good hand to pull material from under the swifts and doffers. He would then put the retrieved fibres through the machine one more time. He never liked ship-shod work or attitudes and I would like to pay warm tribute to him for his workmanship, skills, cheerfulness and loyalty. Bronislaw retired when he 65.

Since writing the above, I have heard from his daughter Wanda that Bronislaw had sadly died in November 2009. He was another good and faithful member of our family business.

Albert Day

Albert came to work with us in the 1970s and was another faithful member of the mill team. In due time he was responsible for the running of the two very large four and five swift machines, Nos.23 and 24, the product from which determined the long-term reputation of our company. These machines processed the finest white botany wool thread wastes which had been prepared then scoured. The prepared material was then garnetted and packed into new 36 inch x 60 inch jute bales for delivery to the West of England for manufacture into surgical and piano hammer felts. Albert did his job well. Our reputation depended particularly on the final product from these

Albert Day 1976

two machines and it is true that there was no other firm which could produce such a fine quality product free of any contamination. For the specific end use of the garnetted wool it was essential that no coloured fibre was present. If there was, we knew (and expected) that the complete delivery would be rejected.

We worked for perhaps five or six waste merchants who trusted us to do this work and because of our high standards we were specified as the processor by the felt manufacturer E V Naish Ltd, in Wilton, near Salisbury. Albert Day was one of a long line of employees who did this work. There were a few occasions when we asked him to work in another part of the mill but Albert would then be like a fish out of water, unhappy and confused, so we always returned him to the machines he knew and understood. Albert was another faithful worker on whom I could completely rely.

Albert's wife Ada was a very talented violinist and in the 1970s she was in great demand by the Royal Northern College of Music in Manchester and she would be asked to go there to tutor some of their students. Ada had been born in Canada but after her mother died she had grown up in England, having been brought home by her father.

One day Albert came to see me as Ada wanted to apply for a passport but she had no birth certificate. I contacted the Canadian High Commission in London for their advice and they put me in contact with the authorities who, in their turn gave me the name of the register office for the village of Cam Lakes where Ada was born. In due time a copy of her birth certificate arrived. When he retired we presented Albert with a cheque to enable him to take Ada to Canada but very sadly he died quite suddenly and the journey never took place.

Ivan Zap 1976

Ivan Zap

Ivan was of Russian extraction and another employee who worked for us in the 1970s and 1980s. He was a very strong, stocky young man who spent most of his time working on the small two-swift machines in the area adjoining the Knowles Street warehouse where the William Tatham carding machines had stood in the 1940s. Ivan did not have the easiest time with us because he worked on some of the most difficult material we were ever asked to process. This was often low quality but still expensive alpaca and cashmere fleece which we were asked to process to remove dirt and contrary material to make them more saleable. This we achieved, but at what cost? Those of us involved in the processing had a difficult time coping with the short fibre or 'fly' hanging in the air, making breathing difficult. Although we issued everyone concerned with face masks it was often difficult to insist that they should be worn.

Ivan endured many days working on difficult blends and he seemed content to do the work to which others would object. I would not say we exploited his loyalty but we were certainly grateful that someone was prepared to perform this unpleasant task. He left us in the early 1990s and the last I heard he was working at a wholesale butchers company somewhere in Bradford.

Jimmy Gould

J immy, in the nicest possible way, was someone I would describe as looking like a character in a painting by Brueghel. He had a large mop of unruly hair and always looked fairly untidy. By the time he came to work with us in the mid 1960s, he had neither his own teeth, nor any dentures.

He had a loud voice, probably because of long exposure to a noisy work place. For much of his time he worked in No.1 shed which the company had originally occupied in 1895. He always walked very briskly and was a conscientious worker. I believe he had been married but I remember him as living alone in a flat at the bottom of Knowles Lane, No.111, as I recall.

Often during his working day he had his own little business making and selling sandwiches for his workmates. To feed himself I have seen him tear a loaf of bread in half, long ways, butter the two halves and eat them with no other filling. His alcohol capacity was legendary and on special occasions, particularly at the beginning of holidays, he would disappear into the De Lacey pub opposite the mill with his wage packet and re-emerge a couple of hours later cheerfully inebriated.

I have no memory of when he left us but I believe his excesses finally caught up with him necessitating his retirement from work. We never had any problem with his

Jimmy Gould fettling a garnett machine 1976

work commitment and I do not think I ever had a cross word with him. He appeared content with his limited lot. He died in the 1980s and when I remember Jimmy I do so with a gentle smile.

Arthur Padgett and Joe Smith

I have only slight memories of Arthur and Joe as they had retired in the early 1950s before I started going regularly to the mill. They usually worked on the Wm Tatham 'preparing' machine in that rather dark area below the street level of the Prince Street yard just outside the wash-house where the natural fibre blends were scoured. The cut material would be piled on the floor above in its constituent layers and then pushed down through a trap door in the floor to where Joe would feed his machine.

The quantity in the blends was usually so large that there was barely room to stand and sometimes Joe would struggle to keep his feet as he threw the 'waste' on to the feed sheet. The coarse, strong teeth of the swift would pull the threads apart as the equally coarse teeth of the worker rollers strained to do their opening process.

The worker teeth were set in wood and chain driven, the heavy chain jumping and bumping as the lumpy material passed between them and the fast running swift roller. There was no real skill in feeding the machine as it was only necessary to achieve an even amount to avoid the feed rollers from jamming. These were spring loaded to allow some variation of weight of material. At the other end of the machine, Arthur stood in front of the delivery rollers and would continuously bend forward with his arms outstretched and pull the web of fibres away. I can see Arthur now in an almost balletic attitude as he repeatedly did this work. He would then carry great armfuls into the wash-house where Joe Fisher or later Charlie Mason would feed the scouring bowls.

Arthur and Joe worked quietly together for years in this department. They would finish one blend, then lift the wooden covers and fettle the rollers, making sure they removed every fibre which could contaminate the next blend. Arthur was quite tall and always tidy and clean. He was kindly and cheerful to me as a youngster - or so I remember after 60 years.

In appearance Joe was the opposite, quite squat and scruffy and lacking several teeth but also appeared to be cheerful. After he eventually retired in the early 1950s, he would stand outside the bottom Prince Street doors as Dad and I left for home on Saturday lunchtimes and, without a word being spoken, he would give us a wide toothy grin as Dad pressed half-a-crown into his open palm.

George Cunliffe and Joe Schofield

These two employees were shadowy characters who worked for us for many years, permanently on the night shift. I did not get to know them very well as I hardly ever saw them. They were prepared to work on any garnett machine anywhere in the mill and were very useful in that they could help to complete any work that was needed urgently.

Looking back I do not know how we allowed these two men to work independently, five nights a week, in different parts of the mill. It cannot have occurred to us that one might have an accident and be unable to summon help. I do not remember that happening but we certainly would not let that situation occur today.

Each afternoon Fred Smith, the works manager, would write in a blue note book his instructions for the coming night shift. This book was kept on a desk in a dark and dismal corner of the former spinning department and George, as the senior man, would daily read the appropriate note and instruct Joe. That would be the only time that they spoke to each other during the dark hours. They just did not communicate. With hindsight, we should not have let this situation go on, if only for health and safety reasons, but this is how it was.

In later years when I was responsible for the planning of work and the processing, I would occasionally stay on at the end of the day, or return to see how a blend was progressing. Walking into the semi-darkened mill with only a few lights on was a similar situation to finding the abandoned ship the 'Marie Celeste', in that machines would be running but there would be no sign of George or Joe.

Eventually they would emerge out of the shadows and confirm that all was well. It was difficult to have a conversation with them as they were so completely self-contained. When George retired Joe went too and we discontinued the night shift.

Fred Foster and Freda Foster

Father and daughter Fred and Freda both worked for us for some time. Fred took over as wagon driver in the 1970s when Wilson Hool retired from driving and Fred too served us cheerfully and well. On one occasion, Stanley Jessop made me some new wooden window frames

Fred and Freda Foster 1980

and he and Fred delivered them to Ilkley on the wagon. The frames were needed at the back of the house and Stanley and Fred carried the largest and heaviest at an angle across the front lawn. Unseen by Fred, there was a large plastic paddling pool full of water on the grass and he manfully stepped into it, walked the full length and stepped out at the other end. Sadly I was not there to hear his watery comments!

Freda worked in the cutting department and eventually she became another Mrs Jessop through marrying Stanley's nephew.

Alan Dickinson

Alan has been a faithful employee for many years. He worked in several areas of the mill and particularly in the preparing area. In the late 1980s, to thank him for his hard work and loyalty, I sent him on two occasions to spend a week at John Ridgeway's Outward Bound School in the far north-west of Scotland where he had experience of ocean sailing and mountain walking.

Alan was always prepared to go the extra mile and help us to overcome any emergency, working many hours of overtime to complete an urgent order. During one particularly unfortunate period when the value of scrap metal was high, many Bradford mill buildings were the target of lead thieves and roofs were regularly stripped overnight. Our premises were no exception and Stanley Jessop was constantly repairing the damage caused and replacing the precious metal with roofing felt. Alan often helped me by standing guard on the premises to try to catch the thieves. We had a special arrangement with the police who promised to come quickly if we called them for help. One late evening, Alan rang for assistance and police cars and officers arrived to arrest several thieves who were on the roof. A police dog handler arrived too and asked Alan if he would hold the animal's lead whilst the officer assisted his colleagues.

The Alsatian dog appeared to be nearly as big as a Shetland pony and was quite animated, obviously wanting to help. As the policeman disappeared into the darkness he said to Alan "Just hold the strap but don't look at him straight in the eyes and don't try to stroke him!" It was a great relief to Alan when the handler returned and relieved him of his agitated charge. Sadly Alan has recently had an accident at the mill and is now not working. I wish him well and hope he has a happier future.

Alan Richmond, left, and Alan Dickinson, right, dismantling the FOR carding machine 2009

Alan Richmond

Alan is one of several members of his family who have worked at the mill over the years. At various times we have employed Alan's father Trevor, who was with us for a long time, his brother Tommy and his sister Susan. In many ways the Richmond family has made its mark on the company. Alan is now an integral part of the processing work and is highly valued.

Right: André Morel the representative of Laroche, S.A. the French builders of textile processing machinery from whom we bought our first Laroche waste pre-opening machine in 1968 (above).

No.23 Four-swift & breast garnett machine used to process the 'fine' white botany threads for the surgical and piano hammer felt trade

Cleaning the BWP scouring bowls

The Customers

I was often asked during my working years what our company did and how did our processes fit into the natural progression of textile manufacture, starting from a natural fleece at one end and a yarn or a finished cloth at the other?

I explained that in a basic sense our company was off the mainstream of textile processing in that the business was similar to a dry-cleaning company in that customers would bring material to us to be improved and value added and we would make a charge for the process. We never owned any of the material we processed.

For example, we worked for spinners who would send us threads that had been discarded and had reduced value and we would return the same material in a valuable form that could be re-used by blending it with new material. In a similar way, the waste merchants were the middle men between the manufacturer and the waste merchants' own customers. We created the added value.

We were not often privy to the end use of the garnetted product but, apart from specialist felts and tennis ball cloth manufacture, huge quantities of dyed, half-prepared woollen material which had been scoured and garnetted by us, was sent to the USA and Canada to be spun into hand knitting yarns. I believe another merchant customer on one occasion supplied our garnetted wool to stuff the axle boxes on the famous locomotive, 'Flying Scotsman'.

Reinhard Hensel, Bradford

Reinhard was a good friend of our company and in a period of over 30 years or more, we must have processed thousands of tons of material for him. He had premises at 112, Thornton Road, near the centre of the city. His front door was at street level and one had to climb a flight of stairs to the first floor and wind past scores of samples to reach his office.

I say 'office' and that is what it was but often one would enter it and not be aware that Reinhard was there. He was a slight man with a small disability as far as walking was concerned but the main reason as to whether one knew he was there or not was that his office was always filled with scores of bags of

Reinhard Hensel

samples. I remember often calling on winter afternoons when a single bulb illuminated the scene. Eventually I would be able to see his diminutive figure crouched over his desk. How Reinhard ever found any particular sample was a continuing mystery, but if one was not easily to hand he would shout at the top of his voice "Cha-a-a-rlie!" and his old retainer and warehouse man would appear from another dim area of the three-storey building to search for the missing package.

Once a year the samples would disappear, his desk and carpet would re-emerge and an element of order would replace the usual utter confusion. I would then know that the annual visit of the accountant was about to take place.

Reinhard had arrived in England from Germany, on his own, in 1938. His relationship with his girlfriend at home was becoming very difficult because she was Jewish. Judy, Reinhard's daughter, told me that her father arrived in London on a Friday afternoon after the banks had closed for the weekend. He was penniless but a kindly landlady took him in and accepted his assurance that he would pay for his accommodation as soon as he had funds. Eventually he arrived in Bradford and we began our long working relationship with him.

Later in 1938, Reinhard's fiancée joined him in Bradford and they were married at the Register Office in Manor Row. They had no one to witness the marriage and so Reinhard went out of the building and asked a complete stranger who was walking past if he would witness the wedding.

After the brief ceremony, the newlyweds took this unknown person to tea at the restaurant in Brown & Muff, the department store. It is true that Reinhard went to sales, probably to John W Pennington's monthly auctions at Shipley, and bought huge quantities of wastes for an eighth of a penny a pound, sorted out the various types and rubbish, then sold the blends on for a farthing a pound, thus making a reasonable profit.

The blends he sent to us did not look as if they were of the highest quality but after our expertise had been used and the many various types had been accurately blended, scoured and garnetted, a miracle usually occurred and the final product would be sold for a surprisingly good price.

Reinhard had a real talent for creating blends and recognising what might be achieved from material others would discard. In the 1960s he exported vast quantities to Africa and Italy. During that time my brother Keith was able to help Reinhard by supporting him as a witness in a court case in Prato in Italy when he was prosecuted about the quality of an exported blend. Eventually the case was dismissed in Reinhard's favour.

I remember Reinhard with great affection. It was rare that we met for a social occasion - perhaps once a year we would take him out for a Christmas lunch - but in my early days at the mill I would visit him, often several times a week, going backwards and forwards to collect and deliver processed samples. We became good friends.

During his final years after he retired, he became confused and existed in his own silent world. Judy tells me that on one occasion she drove him over the moor road from Airedale and as they came down the hill past the Cow and Calf Rocks she said, "This is Ilkley."

Having been silent for many weeks, her father suddenly said, "Roger lives here!" He then returned into his silent existence. Reinhard was another friend whom I remember with great affection. It was a privilege to have known him.

William Playne & Co Ltd
Minchinhampton, Stroud, Gloucestershire

My brother Keith told me that it was during or just after the First World War that we started working for this Gloucestershire woollen mill. Certainly during all my time at the mill you could almost guarantee that every Monday morning a large articulated wagon from Dangerfield's Transport in Stroud would arrive from Minchinhampton with a score of bales of waste.

William Playne's mill manufactured all the fine cloth for Dunlop and Slazenger tennis balls and the waste that they sent was in three types.

The selvedge waste was the strips of cloth cut from the edge of the woven material. The thread waste was the by-product from the spinning or weaving process and comprised large masses of tangled threads, and the third type was the strippings from the carding machines where the blends were first made.

This waste was called 'flights' and was dirty, full of natural grease and chivvy, woody bits from the fleeces. The 'flights', which usually contained up to 15 per cent of grease, needed a really good sort and scour to remove all this foreign material before we could re-card it through a two-swift garnett machine.

The threads and selvedge waste would be prepared, scoured and garnetted and the resulting product was another

A delivery by Dangerfields Transport of tennis ball cloth waste from William Playne & Co 1986

credit to our expertise. When the bales were returned to the Cotswold mill, the blend could be re-blended with new material as a very useful constituent part.

On my fairly regular visits to mills in the south-west I would often spend a comfortable night at the Fleece Hotel in the market square in Cirencester and perhaps have a lunchtime snack at The Woolpack Inn in Slad, up the Cheltenham road from Stroud.

The inn was the favourite hostelry of Laurie Lee the author of that incomparable book about his Cotswold country childhood, 'Cider With Rosie'. Sadly I never met him though his cottage was nearby but I did once play his adult character and narrate his story in a memorable adaptation at Ilkley Playhouse.

I would drive between high hedges and down narrow Cotswold lanes to visit William Playne's Longford Mill which had been on its site since the 1700s. The mill was situated in the bottom of a steep valley through which flowed a small river. The buildings looked as if they had

131

been there for ever and to me it looked as if the whole mill area had evolved organically in its lush green setting.

At one time the mill machinery had been powered by an 'undershot' water wheel where the water disappeared under one of the buildings to re-emerge on the other side. The mill was beautifully built from comfortable, honey-coloured Cotswold stone and on a warm day in summer I used to think that this was an idyllic spot to work, far removed from the greyness of my own West Riding.

Hugh Rose was the friendly wool buyer and spinning manager with whom I had most contact and with whom we worked most closely. Mrs Rose has told me that Hugh was a tower of strength within the company, particularly when little internal disputes occurred. He was always the one to calm things down and sort everything out.

When I called to see Hugh I would drive down the narrow lane from Minchinhampton Common, passing on the right the house where the Playne family had originally lived, and park just outside the mill and in front of an attractive Cotswold cottage. I would make my way up the steps into the office and wait for Hugh in a sunlit room with a large window looking back up the lane. The window sill would be covered with old copies of the 'Wool Record' and equally ancient magazines of field-sports life in Gloucestershire.

These were normally courtesy visits, as the long-standing business went on month after month, year after year. There was rarely any cause for concern. From our point of view we would sometimes mention the amount of contrary material present in the deliveries particularly in the 'flights'. Sometimes we would find large wooden bobbins that had been thrown in with the thread waste from one of the spinning sheds. Often Hugh would tell me of his latest sailing adventure with his wife Freda on his beloved canal narrow boat. I remember on one occasion he told me they brought their boat all the way from the Cotswolds to a gathering at the marina in Leeds. I believe this journey took about three weeks and involved following the canal and river systems all the way from the West of England, finally arriving in Leeds via the Leeds/Liverpool Canal. Hugh could not spare all that time away from Longfords Mill, so Freda completed much of the journey on her own. The valuable waste from Playne's, with the continuous deliveries coming and going between south and north, comprised one of the major sources of our work for 70 or more years. Eventually in the 1990s, the trade fell away and Illingworth Morris, the then parent company, sold out to an American concern and the waste was no longer recycled. Longfords Mill

Hugh Rose of William Playne & Co

was sold to developers who have now completed a fine scheme to convert all the old mill buildings into desirable houses and apartments. Hugh Rose died in 2005 and Freda told me that he never went back to see the new development. He chose to remember the vibrant old mill as it had been in his time. Mrs Rose also told me that Hugh would have been "tickled pink that mention of him would be put in print". I am pleased to be able to quote a few lines from the tribute paid to Hugh at his memorial service by his friend Peter Boxall who said, "Friendship wasn't difficult to Hugh Rose.

"From wool merchants to lock keepers, from old friends to new, all felt the warmth of his concern. In the wool trade he was a highly respected textile man, known for his knowledge, honesty and straight business dealing. For others, his gentle demeanour and practical Christian beliefs that were part of his personality encouraged friendship."

There is no longer the humming sound of spinning and carding machines in Longfords Mill, nor the clatter of looms with mill folk and wagons coming and going each day, but the river still flows its gentle way down the valley towards Nailsworth.

Longfords Mill 1880s

Ely Garnett & Sons Ltd, Elland

The Ely Garnett company was established in 1864. Our company involvement goes back many years and, after discussing how long that was with my friend James Garnett, it seems that initially most of their waste processing was done by City Waste Pulling Company and A S Whitehead and Co and it was not until the demise in the early 1970s of those companies that we were involved with the Garnett family.

The Elland company bought wastes at various mills in the West Riding and, after sorting, sent many types for processing. The blends included coloured botany threads including tight 'thrums', white wool and nylon thread waste, white cross-bred threads and, most especially, white botany wool thread waste.

Our two, large four-swift with breast machines in No.3 shed were kept just for this fine work and produced beautiful garnetted waste for E V Naish Ltd at Wilton near Salisbury. James Garnett and I worked very closely with John Naish on this material because we knew the quality of material that was required for the high quality surgical and piano white felts which the Wilton concern produced.

We processed similar wastes for other companies such as J H Cockcroft Ltd, situated near the river bridge in Elland, and E M Fleming Ltd. and Adolph Jacobs Ltd in Bradford, but eventually James took the bulk of the work from his competitors as he had access to the right sort of raw material that was needed.

James was the son of Douglas Garnett and they worked with Douglas's brother, Joseph Garnett, and his son, Richard. James always referred to Mr Joseph as 'Uncle Joe'. The office and warehouse were in the middle of Elland and I would often visit the family business with processed samples. The sample room was across the hall from the general office and from there you could go into the main warehouse and sorting room. This area was always full of bales of waste, perhaps two or three high, ready for sorting or in work. The Garnetts employed an old retainer, Tom, who did much of the sorting with help from James and Richard and Mr Douglas.

I do not remember Uncle Joe ever being in there. Standing in the centre of the floor was a large coal-fired cast iron stove which heated the building in the winter months. I remember the iron chimney which took the fumes away glowing red on particularly cold winter days.

I always had a friendly welcome when I called. Uncle Joe was invariably in the main office, assisted by a secretary, Christine. The office had a large central table and there was also a large roll-top desk. On the walls were photos of the founder Ely Garnett and other members of the family.

Uncle Joe Garnett was a bluff, well built West Yorkshireman who said what he thought. His son Richard took after him. Mr Douglas had a gentler, quieter personality - at any rate that is how I remember him. On the sales side Richard and James appeared to concentrate on their own group of customers. With Richard's normal more flamboyant, blunt style I was pleased that my main

*Above: Mr
Douglas, Mr
Joseph, Mr
Richard and
Mr James
Garnett of
Ely Garnett
& Son Ltd of
Elland*

*Right: Mr
James and
Mr Richard
Garnett*

involvement in the company was with James, to whom I would speak several times a week as we planned the processing of the many types of waste that they sent to us.

Often the last call each Friday afternoon would be to James to whom I would give the finished weights of the dozen or so bales that had been collected by the carrier for delivery usually to E V Naish Ltd in the west of England on the following Monday morning.

James and I had a mutual respect for each other in our business dealings because our companies depended so much on each other for continuing work. We were grateful for the blends that James sent us on a regular basis and I am sure Ely Garnett's were grateful that the quality of product we achieved enabled them to secure more orders.

James and I are still in regular contact, though he and his wife Glenny are now living near the sea in Fleetwood in Lancashire. The firm of Ely Garnett and Sons ceased to trade in 1995. In describing the long association with James Garnett and his family business in Elland, it is appropriate next to mention the company with whom both our businesses had a mutual interest for many years.

E V Naish Ltd, Wilton

The name of this company, based in Wilton, near Salisbury, in the west of England was well known to those in the Bradford trade who bought or sold processed textile wastes and noils. The company was founded in 1800 when William Naish began making wool corduroy cloth for the local farming community. By 1850 the firm was using their knowledge of wool to supply piano hammer felt to the growing number of European piano manufacturers.

John Naish, the company chairman, with whom I had close contact during my years in charge of processing, wrote in his own history of the family business that in due course his grandfather, William John Naish, became General Manager and later Managing Director in 1882. It was Elizabeth Vaudrey Naish, W J's stepmother, who assumed overall control at that time until her death in 1901 and who gave her initials to the continuing company name.

The working relationship our company had with E V Naish & Co was a mixture of anxiety and satisfaction. On the one hand, there was always some exhilaration and a good deal of pride in seeing another load of bales of processed white botany thread waste going up Knowles Street en route to Wilton.

The bales invariably contained the finest quality recycled product of this type available anywhere in this country, probably the world, but the anxiety was the on-going responsibility in time, care, and effort to achieve this. We knew the high standard of garnetted waste that John Naish needed and there were no short cuts to achieving this.

Sometimes we would receive bales of waste which, even when processed, we knew would not reach John's necessarily high standard. Our customers would be looking at their overall costs, including the price of the raw material, the processing and the transport to the west of England. Very occasionally, if they thought they could save money by including some lower grade material, some would try, but this was usually an expensive mistake. We would advise the customer of our concern but if they insisted we would go ahead - at their risk! In addition nowadays to producing high quality felts for surgical and chiropodist use, polishing felts and sound-proofing felts for the automotive industry, Naish's were, in my time, also manufacturing piano hammer felts for Bechstein and Steinway, the internationally renowned piano makers. There was no room for error.

Several times over the years John Naish rejected deliveries which we sent to him because of perceived low quality. This could be small amounts of fine, tightly twisted threads which even our processing could not open into a fully fibrous state, or sometimes tiny amounts of coloured flecks were present, both of which would show up in the finished white felt. There was also the risk that, in spite of very careful sorting by the merchant, he would not be aware that white thread had been wound on to a bobbin that still contained coloured threads.

This unhappy situation would not be found until it was processed and the coloured threads would contaminate the whole blend with disastrous consequences. The blend could not be used for white felt and consequently its value would

John Naish of E V Naish Ltd

140

be severely reduced. In this situation it was not unusual for our customer to accuse us of causing the contamination, so it paid us to be extremely vigilant in the initial blending and preparing processes.

I have spoken to John Naish and we have had a cheerful discussion about the old days. He reminded me that on several occasions he had to reject deliveries from one customer because the beautifully garnetted waste contained the occasional grey hair and so could not be used.

We were adamant that the fault was not ours and eventually we sent samples away for analysis and we were pleased to find that the hairs belonged to our customer's cat which was allowed to roam around his warehouse, or sit on the wool as it was repacked for delivery to Wilton.

In the mid 1980s John rang me one day to ask if we could reduce the oil content in the finished product that was delivered to them as an unexpected problem had occurred. I have explained that there was always a percentage of spinning oil, say 3% or 4%, on the threads when they were delivered to us which we would then remove during the scouring process.

After drying we would add up to 3% of a new clean emulsified mineral oil, mostly to control fibre breakage during garnetting and to replace some lost weight. This addition would normally be removed by contact with water in subsequent processing.

For some customers, in addition to the traditional white felt, Naish's produced fully dyed felts in rich scarlet and blue shades when the oil content in our garnetted wool was not too critical. For a purely cosmetic and attractive effect, John was asked to produce a piano felt where just the edge of the felt was dyed. This did not appear too difficult until it was discovered that when the edge was hand-dipped into the dye, because of the oil content still present in the wool, colour migrated into the felt, and instead of a permanent straight edge, an uneven, 'jumpy' line appeared.

By this time there were only one or two merchants selling garnetted waste to Naish's and Ely Garnett & Co were the main suppliers. James Garnett and I tackled this problem and it involved us in continually testing the threads for oil content and scouring some of the wastes twice with special detergents to reduce the offending oil. We had some success with this revised processing but then, over a few months in 1989 and 1990, all this vital work came to an untimely end.

After 70 or 80 years of working for E V Naish, their piano hammer felt trade ceased virtually overnight due to the political upheaval in China following the Tiananmen Square massacre, and the collapse of Communism in Eastern Europe.

Our country also suffered a serious slump in 1990 and 1991 from which our best white botany processing trade did not recover and, sadly, the processing skills we had developed for this type of work during very nearly one hundred years became obsolete too.

On a couple of occasions during the many years I used to call to see John Naish in Wilton, I asked if he would take me into his mill so that I could see how the material we sent him was subsequently processed. It was a fascinating sight to see our wool being further carded into a wedge shaped 'bat' that was then compacted beneath huge wooden hammers which reduced its bulk.

This, with the addition of water and steam, created a hard and densely compressed felt. In the mill there was a Dickensian scene of noise and steam, real industry and practical skills which I suspect, like so many others, have now largely disappeared.

I miss my regular visits to the West Country and meeting John who always offered me a friendly and courteous welcome. He would give me great encouragement by telling me about the orders he had given to the West Riding merchants and would confirm that he had instructed them to use our company, and no one else, for the processing of his blends.

I remember too an enjoyable meeting with John in the mid 1970s in Kettlewell, at the top of Wharfedale. He has been a long-time scout leader in Wiltshire and had brought a group to stay at the scout hostel at Hag Dyke, high-up on the fellside below Great Whernside. James Garnett and I took the opportunity to take our respective fathers to meet John and we all enjoyed lunch together at the Racehorses Inn in the village.

I particularly miss my regular visits to Salisbury and having the opportunity of solitary walks around its ancient streets after dinner.

My wife Barbara and I do return from time to time and we agree that there are few more memorable and magical experiences than to stroll into the Close on a warm, still summer evening and see the incomparable cathedral with its beautiful soaring spire, floodlit against a dark blue sky.

Other Friends

When writing about our employees, I mentioned that, before he joined us, Bronislaw Siedlecki had worked for the City Waste Pulling Company in Birksland Street. This company was run by **Paul Whitaker** with whom, although a business competitor, my father had a close friendship. There was also another company doing similar work, A.S. Whitehead and Co, run by Arthur Whitehead in Eccleshill, on the other side of Bradford.

The three companies decided in the 1940s to form a Bradford Waste Pullers Association where it was agreed annually what charges they would make for the various similar processes they undertook. This was a form of price-fixing which would be frowned on (illegal!) today, but it seems it was accepted for many years, and I am sure local arrangements would be established to secure a particularly attractive order.

During the war years the three companies were never busier because of the need to recycle all wastes. For the sake of convenience it was decided that Whiteheads and City

Waste Pulling would process most of the coloured wastes and our company would concentrate on the white un-dyed wastes. As has been mentioned earlier, this was essential in processing for the sensitive surgical and piano felt trade where just a speck of coloured thread in a bale could cause the whole delivery to be rejected by the felt manufacturer.

I used to enjoy the occasional visit to the City Waste Pulling Co. My particular interest was not to see the processing but to go into the boiler house to see the vertical steam engine that provided the power to run the mill machinery. Steam power has always fascinated me and I can stand for hours just watching those majestic machines toiling smoothly away, fascinated by scores of intricate moving parts and comforted by the warm satisfying smell of hot machine oil.

Paul Whitaker of City Waste Pulling Co

(I have been criticised for missing the sight of some glorious landscape whilst watching the 1914 steam engines powering the "Lötschberg" paddle-steamer as it progressed gently down Lake Brienz in the Bernese Oberland, in Switzerland.)

Paul Whitaker's boiler was scrapped when the mill ceased trading in November 1972. It was, however, a happy bonus when I discovered that

145

Brass nameplate from the steam engine at City Waste Pulling Co

my friend Anne Hardy, Paul's niece, has the brass nameplate that carried her name and had been fixed to that steam engine. It was the same Paul Whitaker, mentioned earlier, with whom in 1946 and 1947 my father travelled to Germany to inspect with others what remained of the German textile industry.

In later years, particularly after my father had the accident which forced him into an overdue retirement, Paul and he renewed a long-time interest in radio-telegraphy and attended night-school classes to learn the practical side of the subject. They and their respective wives, Doris and Molly, always remained close friends.

Over the years, many others have supported the family business. I particularly remember **Frank Monkman Ltd** who specialised in selling exotic 'funny' fibres such as silk and reindeer hair. In one of its uses, we blended reindeer hair with wool as an 'effect' fibre for a ladies skirt material for Marks & Spencer. Monkman's also sent us every year or so several bales of human hair which the company had imported from China. Harry Batty and I usually were given the job of cutting this dull black tangled and valuable material into a more manageable length. The product was used in the tailoring trade to stiffen the lapels of gentlemen's jackets. I understand the poorer Chinese were encouraged to sell their hair to enhance their income and I can confirm that we often found the occasional pig-tail!

Left: Frank Monkman

P A Richterich Ltd sent us vast quantities of white mohair thread wastes for scouring and garnetting through the late Donald Plester who ran their waste department.

Kessler & Co. sent us large blends of white wool wastes to be scoured and garnetted and I was always a little concerned when I delivered samples to their manager, Mr Hudson, in the mill just off Canal Road, hoping that we had achieved a high enough standard for him. Tony Vinette and Michael Payne worked in the Kessler sample room and much later we continued that friendship when they were appointed to Bradford Magistrates' Bench.

Michael Payne, Mr Hudson and Tony Vinette in Kessler's wool & waste merchant's sample room, 1970s

John Wellock & Co, whom I knew first in Bradford and then in Cullingworth, were long-standing customers. Jack and Roy Wellock sent us very large quantities of wool wastes for scouring and garnetting. Many of those blends would be delivered to E V Naish, in Wilton.

E G Allsop & Co, run by my oldest friend Nigel Cottam in Hall Lane, provided us for many years with the empty bales we needed to pack all the material we produced. Most customers used their own 'empties' but to avoid contamination, new or cleaned and reconditioned bales were used and Nigel's firm made them for us out of jute or sometimes woven polypropylene cloth.

This business between the two companies went on year after year and I remember standing in Allsop's yard on scores of occasions, looking up and seeing bundles of bales being thrown down to me and my waiting car from a warehouse door high up in the mill.

Philip Cordingley was the manager of Dudley Hill Post

Office for several years and we took advantage almost every working day of the cheerful service generously given by Philip and his wife Joyce. For many years they were a busy part of our local scene.

Philip Cordingley, the Dudley Hill Sub-Postmaster, and his wife Joyce 2009

Gilbert and Mary Morgan were also part of my daily life at the mill but their special interest was in supporting the inner-man through their pork butcher's shop a short distance away at the top of Dawson Lane. Almost every lunchtime I would walk across and join the cheerful queue to buy a warm pork pie or more often a roast beef sandwich and a Kit-Kat. Also on the menu were 'savoury ducks' a tasty ball of cooked minced pork and spices.

If I was really hungry I could also purchase a slice of home-made tart which came with a selection of fillings. When I was thinking of what I should call this book my

Left: Gilbert Morgan's pork butchers shop in Dawson Lane 1980s

Below: Gilbert and Mary Morgan in their shop Christmas 1983

daughter Beth, remembering my daily lunchtime menu, suggested that an appropriate title would be 'A Piece of Jam'. It could also have been 'A Piece of Mince' or 'A Piece of Apple'!

Gilbert confirms my memory of one Christmas Eve when he told me a customer came into the shop just as it was about to close for the festive holiday. The man had forgotten to buy a turkey and was desperate to take one home to his family.

The only one Gilbert had in his shop was the one he had been keeping for himself and his own family but, ever the shopkeeper, Gilbert sold it to the relieved customer. I do not remember hearing what Mary's reaction was on hearing the news. I have been really pleased to make contact again with Gilbert and Mary who now live in retirement not too far away.

Changes

The original company founded by my grandfather still exists, but within a much more far-reaching organisation. The Davy Group is now under the guardianship of two of my brother Keith's sons, Andrew and Mark. At the present time, two independent companies have been created, Andrew running a merchandising business for textile wastes and Mark in charge of textile waste processing. (Shades of the three brothers in 1895!). I wish them both well.

When I look back now, there was complacency in the British textile industry in the 1960s and 1970s of which we should have been ashamed. For a century, Bradford had been the wool capital of the world and such was the great wealth the industry had created for many companies and families, it was never considered that the situation could change.

Working practices and machinery design and manufacture had not moved with the times and I do not think that the industry realised (or did not want to know) that on the other side of the world and in the subsidised and rebuilt factories of Germany, France, Italy, and Switzerland, new designs were being created apace and more efficient machines were being built. It was hardly noticed or barely considered that what had happened in Lancashire to the cotton industry could happen in Yorkshire. But it did and within a few years the whole industry started to contract as cheaper goods were imported and a new culture of dress and furnishings appeared. For example, it did not help that heaters were being fitted into cars, the consequence being that the heavy woollen overcoats that most men wore in the winter became redundant.

The success of our business, especially between the wars and for some time after that, was largely due to one man, my father, and the respect he enjoyed throughout our section of the textile world for so many years. Dad was always an innovator and would not turn away any new fibre or new idea but would always offer the customer the chance to see if the 'waste' could be processed and turned into a worthwhile and saleable product.

It is a sad reflection now in these so-called enlightened times that many of the textile skills that were apparent in the years I worked in Bradford are no longer there to see. Perhaps many processes are now automated and labour-saving but I shall always remember Horace Giles and his skill in making the same shade of alpaca blends from scores of samples of different colours of raw hair, and Reinhard Hensel's remarkable ability in creating acceptable 10,000kg lots of woollen blends from the most unlikely mixtures of wastes.

I remember, too, being taken into the wool sorting shed of that world famous cloth manufacturer, Crombie's of Aberdeen, and seeing men sitting on high stools in front of a sorting desk, surrounded by several bales of the finest quality Australian Merino greasy wool and watching as the sorter took fingersful of fibre and pull it gently through his fingers as he searched for the finest 100s quality wool, (a measurement of fineness) before sending it on its way for blending, scouring, carding, spinning, weaving and finishing to become one of Crombie's supreme cloths. (For a definition of fibre fineness see the glossary at the end of the book.)

That Aberdeen mill closed and was demolished several years ago. It is not long since I went into the Crombie shop in St James's, London, and asked the young man behind the counter if he could tell me from where the luxurious cloth for the overcoats and suits now came? He could not tell me. Ah me!

On my many business journeys around the British Isles, from T & M Hunter & Co in Brora, 70 miles north of Inverness, to Dartington Hall in south Devon, to visit Mr Williams at Trefriw Woollen Mills in North Wales, it was the gentle saunter through the Cotswold countryside that I enjoyed most.

Driving out of Chipping Norton on the road to Moreton-in-Marsh, I used to visit that most distinctive of mill buildings, William Bliss & Co, with its high chimney of unique design. We never processed much waste for them but I shall always remember the small Great Western Railway branch line that brought the bales of greasy wool into the mill complex and the attractive old general office where the staff still sat on high stools working on sloping wooden desks.

As with many similar properties, the mill closed some years ago and was sold to property developers to be turned into desirable apartments. The chimney, looking like a huge rubber drain plunger, still exists as a reminder of former busier days.

Family Matters

My father had learnt many skills throughout his long working life and was always pleased to be consulted and offer advice on how any particular fibre could be re-used. He was invariably courteous, loyal and friendly and over the years I have often had unsolicited tributes paid to him from those with whom he worked and with whom he competed and often advised and helped.

But, unrecognised by many, including in some instances by his immediate family, he had a sterner side to his business character, particularly in circumstances where he thought someone was not being fair, or was trying to trick him, or being ungrateful.

On one occasion I remember two representatives from the same firm coming up the office stairs to sell belting or detergent or something similar. Dad, on opening his office door and seeing two salesmen said to them, "Good morning, gentlemen, and what is wrong with your product?" In their confusion one of them said "Oh nothing, Mr Davy, why do you ask?" My father replied, with a twinkle in his eye, "Well it takes two of you to sell it!"

It was Dad's usual practice to pay Christmas bonuses to those working in the mill. The amount would reflect his assessment of what positive contribution a person had been made to the running and welfare of the company during the past year. One man came to see him and showed him the cheque he had received and told Dad he had not been given as much as so-and-so had been given. My father took the cheque from him, looked at it, said, "Oh no, you haven't" tore the cheque in half, and gave it back to the unhappy recipient.

I must confess I did not see this happen but the story was told to me by someone in the mill. I can believe that Dad would have given a great deal of thought about how much bonus to pay and who amongst his staff deserved extra thanks. I can also believe that he would have been saddened and disappointed that his generosity rebounded in such a way.

I have wondered, as it was Christmas, if Dad eventually relented, because he was thinking about the man's family, and paid the chap some extra money. It would have been in keeping with his character and he would have paid it out of his own pocket.

Dad was generous in a quiet way. When one of his customers, a Mr Haley, fell on difficult trading times, Dad lent him a sum of money. I am not sure if the amount was ever repaid but I can remember Dad's rather wistful smile every Christmas for several years afterwards when, instead of a cash repayment, a very large box of fruit would be delivered to the office. In spite of the depth of the box the fruit only occupied the top layer but I always enjoyed the Cox's Orange Pippin!

Again, I do not know the circumstances, but my father had an orchid named after him by a professional grower who had a nursery on Westgate Hill. I believe that Dad

Walter and Doris Davy at Waterhead,
Windermere 1968

Orchid
'Walter
Davy'
1950s

had lent the man some money to help him in his business. I have a black and white photo of the bloom, 'Walter Davy', and it is my intention to try through a retired JP friend to recreate the lovely flower.

My father worked far beyond the normal retirement age. He never really believed that either Keith or I could make a success of running the company and, of course, he had never known another way of life. Apart from annual holidays, he was always at the mill and that was his life's focus.

The longest break we had at the mill, except for the annual two week summer holiday in August known in Bradford as Bowling Tide, was the Easter weekend. The mill would close on the evening of Maundy Thursday because, as a committed Christian, Dad did not think it was ever appropriate to work on Good Friday.

Eventually in 1963, because of his accident, he was forced to take a watching brief on events at Dudley Hill and Keith and I were allowed to make changes. Remarkably, Dad had never borrowed money to buy machines. They had always been funded out of income. It caused him much concern when we decided to borrow money from Forward Trust, the loan department of Midland Bank.

Dad did, however, accompany Keith to France to buy our first Laroche opening machine in the autumn of 1967 and in January 1968 I travelled with him by train to Biella in northern Italy to see and order the FOR carding machine. The Laroche machine created a much more pre-opened material without excess fibre breakage and the FOR card was a very large sophisticated high production machine for softer spun wastes particularly for carpet thread wastes.

It was also part of the man that in retirement and right up until his death on 17th April 1979, my father never applied

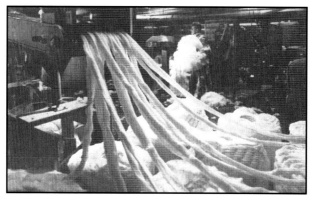

Jimmy Gould cutting synthetic garnetted sliver.

Dennis Walker with the French
'Laroche' pre-opening machine

The Italian FOR carding machine, Wilson Hool left,
Stanley Jessop, right (These photographs were taken
by Barry Wilkinson for the Wool Record and have
been reproduced from cuttings)

159

Keith Davy 2008

Roger Davy in his office 1976

for the old age pension. I suppose it was because of his comparatively modest upbringing where nothing was bought unless the account could be immediately settled.

He considered that the pension was a charity and, although he had paid his income tax and National Insurance throughout his working life, he could not bring himself to accept a weekly payment from the government. I am sure, however, that my mother in later days would have been pleased to use that charity to be able to supplement the heating costs of the family home.

I have considered writing about my brother Keith and his involvement with me and the company. He quite often asked "What you going to say about me?" Sadly, because he has now died and I am still comparatively close to the present day businesses now run by his sons, I think another generation will have to do that in more detail. Enough to say I was grateful for his brotherly support and advice over the years and it was a help when eventually he started his merchandising company as it made it easier, in a declining industry, for two growing families to live out of the extra income this generated.

I am confident that Keith would not have minded (he would probably have been amused) if I mention that Stanley Jessop created a modern wood-lined office for him on the ground floor of the office block. The former sample rooms and stores were converted into smart premises for Keith to receive his visitors and the word went around, on completion, that Stanley, with his funeral director's background, had christened the rather plush area, the 'Chapel of Rest'.

During recent years, Keith and I met in Betty's Cafe in Ilkley on alternate Monday mornings and talked about our days at the mill. There was plenty to talk about and to remember. In October 2009, when KD and I last met there, I had no idea that he would not see the completed version of this narrative.

I am very sorry about this as he encouraged me many times to finish it. After a short period of illness, he died in Harrogate Hospital on the 6th December, 2009. It all seemed too quick and unsatisfactory as he appeared to give up, ultimately contracting pneumonia, and my big brother, without a fuss, just slipped quietly away.

Epilogue

This has been primarily the story of people with whom I worked for many years. Our customers and clients had confidence in the way we did things and they, in their turn, provided us with the work which kept the Company going. For our part, we always strove to do a good and honest job.

For the most part our employees were good and faithful men and women, some of whom reached their potential early in their working careers, appearing to be content with their lot, but serving us well. The work could be hard, dirty and repetitive but that is not unusual in many industries. Although I viewed the life of the company from a position of some advantage, I believe there was generally a good and caring atmosphere.

Now, in 2010, we have a time in Bradford and in the wider world which my father Walter and certainly my grandfather Francis Henry would not recognise. Indeed, there are aspects now which are strange to me. The company, courageously established by the three Davy brothers 115 years ago, still exists but in a vastly different form. I have to confess I am content now not to be a part of it. I had my day, now my nephews must have theirs.

The sights and smells of the past will stay with me for ever.

The loading bay floor at the Knowles Street end of the mill had been heavily reinforced with concrete and redundant tram lines at the beginning of the Second World War to create an air raid shelter and large steel girders supported the floor from underneath.

It was easy to walk down a slight slope under the loading bay through a bomb-blast-proof passage into an open area lit by two single bulbs where the whole workforce could assemble if necessary. Auxiliary firemen's jackets, helmets and axes hung there on the walls in case of need but I do not think the area was used very often.

In this place in my day there was always a mixture of the sadly acrid yet sweet smell from adjacent drains. In this dank, dark area stacks of grey Welsh slates from the roofs of our demolished cottage properties were stored, together with fetid piles of partly decomposed brown jute bales, the unused relics of long forgotten blends.

I remember the heat of the boiler house where the huge vertical Cochran boiler stood, raising steam to warm the entire mill and the scouring department. During the summer holiday, at Bowling Tide, the hinged boiler doors were opened and the steam pipes swept clean with long wire brushes.

On a few occasions, when the boiler inspector was due for his annual visit, I actually went inside the boiler through the narrow inspection hatch on the top rim to see for myself where the engineers had been removing the accumulated water scale from the edge of the domed interior.

It was a dark, rather scary, claustrophobic experience and I can still hear the muffled sound of Dennis Walker inside using his wire brush and hammer. Because our Bradford water was so soft this essential work was only needed once a year. I usually went to the mill on Saturday mornings and as a weekly treat would go to Ada's Café, the wooden hut on the roadside at Dudley Hill which sold excellent bacon sandwiches, to buy enough for everyone working that day including myself. That little café was a local institution and probably these days would not pass all the food hygiene and health and safety regulations.

The bacon was cooked on a gas stove in a very large, deep-sided frying pan which was bubbling with hot fat a few millimetres from the rim. Eventually, after many years service to the community, I was sad to hear that the café had suffered a catastrophic fire and never re-opened. They really were the best of bacon sandwiches.

My family have told me that I must mention the day I was going up the narrow wooden staircase to the first floor of the Imperial building. I used to say to myself that I should always run up two steps at a time to demonstrate I could still do it. On this particular occasion I was so enthusiastic and my arms were moving so fast that I punched myself very hard in the face and saw stars for several minutes, a rather embarrassing experience for a grown man.

On the debit side, amongst other traumas across the years, I remember one winter's day when I struggled from home to drive through deep snow for three hours to find the office block had been burgled overnight and all the rooms resembled a battlefield. The safes had been overturned and one that only contained documents had its back ripped off. Cupboards had been rifled and their contents scattered and powdered coffee liberally distributed over the entire area. I just sat in shock, without moving for an hour or more, and contemplated the sad scene.

Another morning in the early 1980s, soon after we

bought the adjoining premises of the defunct dye-house of W & G Chamber's, I was greeted by Dennis Walker with the word "Disaster!" He told me a considerable piece of the 120ft mill chimney, included in the sale, had collapsed during the night and fallen through the roof of No.1 shed. Thankfully, it had been during the dark hours, because if anyone had been working beneath we would have had fatalities. We were forced to employ a specialist firm of steeple jacks to 'drop' the rest of the stack to make it safe - a costly exercise which we could ill afford.

When I see any mention of viscose, or artificial silk as my father would always call it, I think of our No.2 shed where in my younger days we ran eight smaller 2-swift garnett machines specifically for processing synthetic fibres, far away from any natural fibres. We were probably one of the first commission processors to recycle synthetics. Viscose was a real problem in that it is made from one hundred per cent cellulose derived from spruce trees and it is a highly inflammable material.

As the half-opened waste passed through the machine, it would take only a tiny piece of unseen metal to catch on a wire-covered roller to cause a spark which ignited the fibre and, whoosh! There would be a mighty conflagration in the area, the water sprinklers above would be activated and, hopefully, quickly extinguish the fire. Eventually our insurers said enough was enough and refused adequate cover for the risks involved, so we stopped processing viscose. In many ways it was a great relief.

One day in the late 1950s our wagon collected a new cutting machine which had been delivered to a depot in Bradford from the manufacturer in Germany. Wilson Hool reversed his wagon into the Prince Street yard and the crane rope was attached to the large wooden crate containing the machine. The whole package probably weighed two tons and all went well until we were just about to swing the crate into the crane door three floors above the yard.

Suddenly the crane mechanism failed and the crate fell down and hit the wagon body so hard that the back was broken. The wagon took some weeks to repair and the new machine was not serviceable until new spare parts were received. Eventually we used a large mobile crane to land the machine safely. The only consolation was that on the first occasion Wilson had had the foresight not to be standing underneath.

I shall always be grateful that I was given the opportunity to work with the fitter who came to build the new Italian FOR carding machine during the summer of 1968. The huge machine, which was 2.5 metres wide and had two very large main swift rollers also 2.5 metres in diameter, arrived on two containers from Biella in northern Italy.

Because of its size and the lack of headroom we had to create a large pit so that the swifts could be accommodated partly below floor level. As the top soil was removed, we soon discovered a large seam of coal about two feet thick which was also removed across the width of the hole. In the mill's early days the boiler fires were fed from coal dug from an open-cast mine at the bottom of Knowles Street and there must have been coal beneath many factories around.

This beautiful machine was used to card acrylic lap waste and carpet thread waste and was built like a Rolls-Royce car. It had not been erected in Biella before it was delivered to Bradford. That was the confidence the makers had in their product and Livorno, the fitter, and I built it together in about six weeks. In erecting that huge machine, not one item was missing and every part fitted so exactly that we never once had a reason to use a file. Sadly, 40 years later I understand that beautiful machine became surplus to requirements and has been dismantled, mostly with a heavy hammer and sold for scrap.

Now I have reached a time in retirement when there is no need to dwell too long on the anguish I suffered in the early 1990s when yet another recession in the textile industry hit us very hard. We had little work coming in from our customers who were also struggling to obtain orders and we had a much reduced income with which to pay our staff.

I was forced to make some of our people redundant, always a dreadful experience when I knew what personal commitments they had to their own families. Every working day for weeks on end our bank manager would ring to see if we had received any cheques in the post and, if not, he would forcefully enquire what I was going to do about the critical situation.

There was little I could do, our customers were not being paid either. No doubt the manager had responsibilities as well to his own superiors but I shall always find it difficult to forgive the unreasonable pressure he put on me and our long established company. We survived, unlike many of our faithful customers, but it was close run thing.

It is of some comfort for me to know that the traditional work produced in our family textile business for over one hundred years has been of such high quality and that although times have changed and processes disappeared, the family name still exists as one of the few survivors of the Bradford trade.

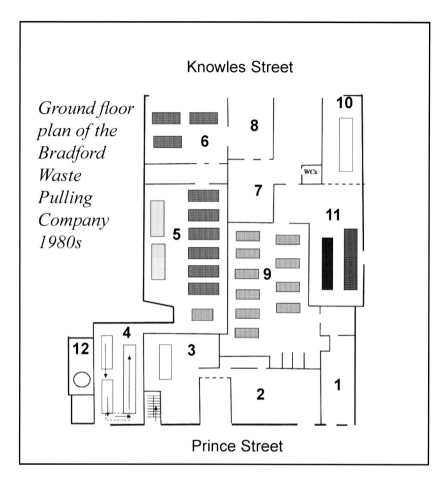

Ground floor plan of the Bradford Waste Pulling Company 1980s

Knowles Street

Prince Street

1 Office block 2 Imperial works
3 Three-storey warehouse including 'Laroche' room and precision cutting area
4 Three storey warehouse, scouring on the ground floor 5 The original 'Anchor' or No.1 shed, Garnett machines 6 Carding and, later, garnetting room and joiner's shop above
7 Outgoing warehouse 8 Outgoing warehouse
9 No.2 shed for synthetic garnetting
10 No.3 shed and Italian 'FOR' carding machine
11 No.3 shed and best white garnetting machines
12 Boiler house

Acknowledgements

My particular thanks to Fredrik Bagge of Karlstad, Sweden (left) for many of the black and white portraits which he took when working in the mill in 1976

My thanks also to

The City of Bradford Museums and Galleries for aerial photos of Bradford.

Ian Mackintosh of the Stroudwater Textile Trust in Gloucestershire for the photo of Longfords Mill in the 1880s.

The Fleetwood Maritime Heritage Trust for use of the photo of my father's ship.

Many friends and former business associates and relatives of those who have been part of this story, who have supplied photos to supplement the narrative.

My brother Peter Davy of Hartley, Kirkby Stephen, Cumbria, who has encouraged me and helped me with some editing.

My wife Barbara for her love, support and encouragement throughout my working years and since, and for allowing me to use her 1980s pastel painting of what was the original Anchor Shed for the book cover.

And finally to my publisher Caroline Brannigan for all her advice and cheerful support.

Glossary

Bale Cart: A strong, low, often wooden, two-wheeled trolley for moving bales.

Blend: Various fibre components ultimately processed into a unified form.

Carding: The process of separation and mixing of fibres as a preparation for spinning.

Clip: Pieces of cloth rejected during manufacture or when making a garment.

Cutting: The mechanical reduction in length of wool sliver or tangled thread wastes before blending.

Doffer: The slow-running roller on a carding or garnett

machine which removes the fibres from one working part of the machine and delivers it to the next or finally removes the carded material via a toothed doffing comb at the end of the process.

Droppings: The short fibres, often almost dust, which 'drop' from the working parts of a carding or garnett machine during processing.

Fatty matter: The natural oil content contained in a wool fleece or animal hair.

Fettle: A colloquial textile term to completely clean a machine.

Finely clothed: On a garnett machine the working points of the rigid wire covering the rollers may have many points per inch/cm across their width. The initial rollers are often coarsely clothed.

Fibre fineness: The mean fibre diameter which is usually expressed in microns which is a unit of measurement used in assessing the diameter of a fibre. A micron is equal to one millionth of a metre.

Flights: The greasy, dirty, coarse fibres containing seed or 'shivvy' wooden bits, removed from the card wire during 'fettling', see above.

Fly: Short dusty material present in the air during various textile processes.

Four swift with breast: The possible constituent working sections of a large garnett machine. The 'breast' is usually an initial coarse-wire covered fast-running roller which follows the feed rollers.

Garnett: The company, P&C Garnett Ltd of Cleckheaton, West Yorkshire, gave its name to a textile process. Their machines were specifically designed for processing textile wastes.

Garnetting: The process, using a garnett machine, which may have several working sections, to reduce a thread from its twisted, spun state into a fully opened fibrous state so the fibre may be re-used.

Gill box: The gill box is designed to straighten, draw-out and level carded sliver before combing.

Harrow: Long pointed metal teeth on a shaft, moving in an ellipse across the width of the bowl and dipping down into the scouring liquor and used to progress material through a scouring machine.

Knotter/Rag machine: A fast-moving, single swift, coarsely clothed machine for the pre-opening of fine twisted and tangled strong waste or clip.

Lanolin: The wool fat which is removed in initial scouring which has been the traditional basis of many ointments and creams.

Laroche: A sophisticated modern French built machine used by our company to pre-open wastes. We bought the second UK imported machine in 1968.

Noil: Short wool fibre cast out as waste in combing wool for worsted 'fine' yarn.

Opening machine/Pre-opener: Eg a 'knotter' or 'Laroche', see above.

Preparing: The process of pre-opening wastes for scouring and/or garnetting.

Ramie: A vegetable textile fibre.

Scouring: The washing and cleaning and subsequent drying of natural textile animal fibre eg wool, mohair, alpaca, camel hair.

Selvage/Selvedge: The strong edge of a woven cloth, produced to prevent unravelling or fraying.

Skep: A wooden or wicker constructed container, sometimes with a hinged lid, on wheels or sleds.

Swift: The fast-running working part of a carding or garnett machine revolving in very close proximity to the slow running 'worker' rollers which run in the opposite direction and between which the fibres or threads are momentarily held by the respective wire points and progressively opened.

Shoddy: Inferior fibres made from, for example, shredded old clothing or rags.

Sliver: A condensed 'rope' of fibres, eg a wool top consists of a large ball of wound sliver.

Thrum(s): Tightly knotted threads often from where the warp threads have been attached to the warping beam.

Warp: Threads stretched lengthwise in a loom to be crossed and interwoven by the weft.

Weft: The cross threads carried by a shuttle across the width of the loom to create a cloth.

Woollen: A slightly coarser hairier cloth, eg Harris Tweed or blankets, where in manufacture no attempt is made to make the fibres lie parallel to each other.

Wool tops: The combed wool which contains the longest and straightest fibres which form the basis of a worsted thread.

Worker: A smaller diameter slow moving roller set in very close proximity to the fast running swift where the working action takes place. On a garnett machine there can be up to eight workers around the periphery of the swift.

Worsted: Smooth highly valued wool cloth particularly used in gentlemen's suitings. Often these days the cloth may consist of a wool /synthetic fibre blend.